Spice for Life

Spice for Life

Delicious Recipes Using Everyday Healing Spices

Instructables.com

Skyhorse Publishing

Skyhorse Publishing books may be purchased in bulk at special discounts for sales promotion, corporate gifts, fund-raising, or educational purposes. Special editions can also be created to specifications. For details, contact the Special Sales Department, Skyhorse Publishing, 307 West 36th Street, 11th Floor, New York, NY 10018 or info@skyhorsepublishing.com.

Visit our website at www.skyhorsepublishing.com.

10 9 8 7 6 5 4 3 2 1

Library of Congress Cataloging-in-Publication Data is available on file.

ISBN: 978-1-5107-0396-4
Ebook ISBN: 978-1-5107-0397-1

Printed in China

Table of Contents

Introduction

Spices provide just the right touch to each meal. A pinch here and a dash there are all you need to create an amazing dish! In Healing Spices the Instructables community shows you how turmeric, ginger, garlic cloves, and many other spices can add just what you need to kick your meals up a notch.

First, we'll start you off with the basics on different types of spices, and how to use them to get the most out of your meal. Find out which spices will help you lower blood pressure and which have antibiotic qualities. Then start letting your culinary creativity run wild with Ginger Carrot Soup, followed by Chicken Tikka Masala with Turmeric Rice, and rounded off with Gingered Hot Pepper Jelly for dessert.

Spices do much more than provide tasty dishes, you can also use them outside of the kitchen. We've also included recipes that act as natural remedies to illnesses and ways to enhance beauty products. Learn how garlic can cure your ailments and how you can combine cinnamon, nutmeg, and honey for smoother skin! Whether you are looking to spice up your meal or spice up your life, Healing Spices has what you need!

Nicole Smith (Penolopy Bulnick)

Natural Remedies (Herbs and Spices)

By Peter11235

www.instructables.com/id/Natural-remiedies-herbs-and-spices/

Using medicines all the time (if they are not necessary) may harm you because they make your immune system weaker. A better alternative is using natural things that don't get rid of diseases but boost your immunity so you can deal with medical conditions by yourself. I will share some of my knowledge about such things in this instructable. WARNING! If you get ill, go to a doctor. This can HELP to prevent/heal some diseases, but when you are ill, the doctor's knowledge will be a better bet than herbs and spices. If you don't listen, it's on your own responsibility and not mine.

Step 1: Cinnamon, cloves, basil, bay leaf, ginger and rosemary

Cinnamon Helps to prevent diabetes (lowers amount of sugar in blood by 25% for at least 2 hours)

Cloves Lower the cholesterol and amount of sugar in the blood. They also reduce high blood pressure and help with digestive system problems. And they are anti-toxic.

Basil Helps to prevent all kinds of cancer.

Bay leaf Anti-diabetes. Helps to regenerate muscle tissue and helps to regenerate after training.

Ginger This is an amazing one. It improves immunity, eases asthma problems, helps with sleep disorders, is antitoxic, antibiotic, anti-pain, anti-hangover, anti-motion/seasicknes, and anti-cold. It adds energy, and improves concentration and working of nervous system. It can warm you up, improves blood circulation, and lowers cholesterol.

Rosemary Antitoxic, anti-headache, anti-rheumatism. Improves memory and strenghtens overall health.

Step 2: Garlic, paprika, pepper, and oregano

Garlic Is a strong antibiotic and helps to prevent breast and intestinal cancers. It keeps its healing properties even after being boiled/baked.

Paprika Contains vitamin C. It also helps with losing weight (speeds up metabolism and fat loss). It also helps with digestion.

Pepper Lowers blood pressure and is good for the digestive system. It strenghtens the healing effects of other spices, herbs, and antibiotics.

Oregano Helps prevent cancer. Antifungal, antibacterial, antiparasitic. It relaxes, helps to prevent colds, and helps with sleeping disorders.

Step 3: Honey, green tea, conifers, mint, and turmeric

Honey Antibiotic. Fun fact: Honey found in pharaohs' tombs is still edible.

Green Tea Good for your heart. Helps to prevent cancer and tooth decay.

Conifers Antitoxic and antibiotic. Produce oils that evaporate into air, so simply being in the woods can improve your health.

Mint Helps to prevent and heal problems with the digestive sytem (mint tea). Relaxes. Antiviral, antitoxic, anti-stress, and anti-pain.

Turmeric Helps prevent Alzheimer's and cancers. Helps heal wounds, cleans blood, and aids with digestive system problems.

Soups

- Pumpkin Soup
- Ginger Carrot Soup
- Roasted Garlic Soup
- Sweet Potato and Coconut Soup

Pumpkin Soup

By James Williamson

www.instructables.com/id/Creamy-Pumpkin-Soup/

This soup is great at the time of year when the days are getting colder and everyone's scooping out all that fantastic pumpkin goop to carve their Jack-o-lanterns! It's warming, creamy, nutritious, and really tasty! Once made, it keeps great in the fridge for up to five days. It also freezes really well, and if frozen in blocks it takes up less space than a skinned chopped pumpkin.

I added a small amount of cumin to give it warmth and add to the flavor of the pumpkin. This recipe's also fantastic with butternut squash and good with any other squash.

Pumpkins are in season from September onwards.

Step 1: Ingredients

- 2 onions
- 4 tbsp. olive oil
- 1 kg pumpkin or squash flesh (mine was of a medium size; it weighed 1,600 g before chopping up and 900 g after. Small pumpkins tend to be the tastiest.)
- ½ tsp. cumin
- ¼ tsp. turmeric (optional)
- 2 garlic cloves
- 2 vegetable stock cubes
- 500 ml boiling water
- 150 ml heavy cream
- Dash of pepper

Step 2: The Onion

Finely chop the onions. Heat the olive oil on low heat in a large pan. Add the onions and sauté until they're soft, not brown.

Step 3: Prepare the Pumpkin

Lop off the top and bottom of your pumpkin to make it more stable, then divide it down the middle. Scoop out the seeds and save them. They're great roasted. Mine was a fresh, young pumpkin from my garden, so the skin was still very thin. A peeler did the job of removing the skin. If yours is slightly older or bigger, you may need to shave it off with a sharp knife. Cut the two halves of the peeled pumpkin into evenly sized cubes.

Step 4: Add the Pumpkin

Add the pumpkin to the pan. Sauté with the onion for about 10 minutes or until the flesh becomes darker and begins to soften.

Step 5: The Spice Must Flow!

Add the cumin and turmeric. My pumpkin wasn't particularly orange, so I decided to add the quarter teaspoon of turmeric to give it some color. Sauté the pumpkin and onion with the spice for five more minutes.

Step 6: Garlic and Stock, then Simmer

Finely chop the garlic and crumble the stock cube, then add them to the pan. Pour in 500 ml boiling water. Cover and simmer on medium-low heat for 20–30 minutes or until the pumpkin is soft. Stir occasionally.

Step 7: Cream It!

Turn down the heat and add 150 ml heavy cream and a dash of pepper. Stir it in, bring the soup to a low boil, then turn off the heat.

Step 8: Blend and Season

I used a hand blender straight in the pan so I could blend it while it was still hot. Alternatively, allow to cool slightly then pour into a blender or food processor. Taste the soup. You may need to add a little salt or more pepper to taste.

Step 9: Serve

Add a sprig of parsley on top and serve piping hot with buttery toast or crusty rolls. Enjoy!

Ginger Carrot Soup

By canida
www.instructables.com/id/Ginger-Carrot-Soup/

This is a simple, quick, and tasty winter soup.

Prep time: About 10 minutes

Cook time: 30–45 minutes

Step 1: Ingredients

- 1 pound carrots (shredded)
- ½ large onion (shredded)
- 1 bouillon cube + water (or substitute with stock or broth)
- Several chunks of ginger (depending on your taste)
- Bay leaf
- Fresh ground black pepper to taste
- 2 tbsp. coconut milk (optional)

Step 2: Cooking

Shred carrots and onion, then place in a pot. Add water until the vegetables are just covered. Add bouillon cube, ginger, bay leaf, and pepper. Simmer soup on low until vegetables are cooked through and most of the water has evaporated. Taste and adjust seasonings; add coconut milk if desired. Remove bay leaf and ginger chunks and serve.

Scaling this recipe is easy! I used four pounds of carrots (approximately seven cups shredded) and two onions with four bouillon cubes and a big handful of ginger.

Roasted Garlic Soup

By wold630

www.instructables.com/id/Roasted-Garlic-Soup/

Ah, the time of year when everyone seems to be sniffling and sneezing. Since garlic is oh so tasty and a natural antibiotic, it is a match made in heaven. This soup will clear the sinuses while tasting great!

Step 1: Chicken Stock

Every great soup starts with a great base—in this case, homemade chicken stock. You can substitute store-bought stock if you prefer, but if you have the time and resources you should really make your own. You won't regret the extra effort, especially when you warm the whole house with the savory aroma of roasted chicken and vegetables and taste the difference in the end product.

Homemade Chicken Stock:

- 4 chicken thighs–bone in (very important)
- 6 cloves garlic
- 1 onion, sliced
- 4 large carrots, quartered
- Salt and pepper

Preheat oven to 350°F.

Add all ingredients to an appropriately sized roasting pan, making sure fat side of chicken is up. Salt and pepper generously.

Bake 45–60 minutes or until chicken reaches 165°F.

Remove pan from oven and let chicken cool until you can pull all of the meat off the bone. Reserve for a later meal.

Add all chicken bones, fat, and veggies to a large stock pot and fill with one quart of water. Bring to a boil, reduce heat, cover, and simmer about 45 minutes.

Using a large, fine-mesh colander, strain liquid into a large bowl and set aside.

Eat the carrots because you can't resist and discard the rest.

Step 2: Roast Garlic

Preheat oven to 350°F.

Cut the top off one head of garlic. Drizzle with olive oil and place in a garlic roaster.

Roast 45–60 minutes or until garlic is tender.

Let cool then squeeze out the garlic into a small bowl. Set aside.

If you don't have a garlic roaster, wrap the garlic loosely in aluminum foil instead. You will get the same result.

Instead of having the oven on twice, you can roast the garlic at the same time as the chicken if you are making stock.

Step 3: Make Soup

Roasted Garlic Soup:

- 1 head garlic, peeled and sliced
- 1 large onion, diced
- 2 tbsp. olive oil
- 1 head roasted garlic
- 1 quart chicken stock
- ⅓ cups milk
- 1 small potato, peeled and diced
- 2 oz. cream cheese
- 2 tbsp. butter
- Salt and pepper

Garnish (optional):

- Scallions, thinly sliced
- Parmesan cheese, shredded
- Croutons

In a large soup pot, sauté garlic and onion over medium-high heat with olive oil until translucent. Add in roasted garlic, chicken stock, milk, potato, and cream cheese. Bring to a boil. Reduce heat to a simmer and cover. Continue simmering 10–15 minutes or until potatoes are tender.

Using an immersion blender, blend the soup until smooth. Return to low heat. Add butter, and then salt and pepper to taste.

Serve hot and garnish with scallions, cheese, and croutons if desired.

Sweet Potato and Coconut Soup

By Tim Fulford

www.instructables.com/id/Sweet-Potato-and-Coconut-Soup/

This is a creamy, slightly sweet, warming soup that is really easy to make and takes less than 30 minutes.

Step 1: Ingredients

- 2 tbsp. olive oil
- 2 cloves of garlic, crushed
- 1 onion, finely chopped
- 2 pinches of chili flakes
- 2 pinches of ground ginger
- 400 g of sweet potato, peeled and chopped
- 400 ml of chicken or vegetable stock
- 200 g creamed coconut
- 50 g fresh coriander leaves, chopped (optional)
- Salt and pepper to taste
- Coriander or spinach to garnish

Step 2: Heat Oil

Heat the olive oil in a large sauté pan, then add the garlic and onion. Gently sauté for 3–4 minutes, or until soft and golden brown.

Step 3: Add Spices and Sweet Potato

Once the onion and garlic are cooked through, add the chili flakes and ground ginger, sautéing for another 2–3 minutes. Then add the sweet potato and cook for 2–3 minutes.

Step 4: Add the Stock and Coconut

Now add the stock (hot) and coconut. Allow to cook for about 10 minutes. Take care when adding hot liquid to a hot pan. At this stage, if you wish to add the optional chopped coriander leaves, then do so.

Step 5: Remove from Heat

Remove from the heat and allow to cool before pouring into a blender or food processor. Beware of adding hot liquids to a blender. Hot liquids can scald!

Blend until it has a smooth and even consistency. You might find that you need to add a little warm water to thin it out, but this is entirely up to you.

Step 6: Get Ready to Enjoy

Reheat or store in freezer. If you are going to freeze the soup, then it is essential to let the soup reach room temperature before putting it in suitable containers and freezing.

Season to taste and garnish with coriander (or anything green) and serve with homemade crusty bread. It's really quite delightful.

Sides, Breads, and Condiments

- Cinnamon Simple Syrup
- Delicious Red Onion Chutney
- Fresh Turmeric and Persimmon Chutney
- Orange, Fig, and Sage Chutney
- Garlic Bread
- Cayenne Toasts
- No-Flour Cinnamon Blueberry Pancakes
- Spicy Mocha Popcorn

Cinnamon Simple Syrup

By Nicole Smith

www.instructables.com/id/Cinnamon-Simple-Syrup/

Simple syrup is really handy to have around. It's great during the colder months to sweeten up hot beverages. I decided to make a cinnamon simple syrup for something a little different.

Step 1: Ingredients

- 1 cinnamon stick (add more for a stronger flavor)
- 1 cup water
- 1 cup brown sugar

Step 2: Recipe

Add all ingredients to a saucepan and cook to a boil. Then simmer for 10 minutes or so. Remove from heat and let it cool. Store with cinnamon stick if you desire.

Delicious Red Onion Chutney

By Jan Wante

www.instructables.com/id/Delicious-red-onion-chutney/

Onions are my favorite vegetables. They come in I don't know how many varieties, and there are thousands of great recipes to use them in. Here is one of my favorites: red onion chutney.

Step 1: Ingredients

- 1 kg red onions
- 30 g butter
- 220 g cane sugar
- A pinch of ground cinnamon
- 2 cloves
- 150 ml raspberry vinegar
- 350 ml red wine
- A pinch of salt
- Some pepper

Step 2: Instructions

Chop the onions as fine as you like and glaze them in the butter. Add the sugar, the cinnamon, and the cloves and let it caramelize for about 15 minutes.

Add the vinegar, the wine, the salt, and the pepper and boil it without a lid until it is reduced to a thick mass (it will take about 15 to 20 minutes).

Put it in jars and store it in a cool place.

This recipe tastes excellent with all kinds of meat and game.

Fresh Turmeric and Persimmon Chutney

By Kathleen Stringer

www.instructables.com/id/Fresh-Turmeric-and-Persimmon-Chutney/

Step 1: Ingredients

- Fresh turmeric root, about a pound or 3–4 cups, unpeeled
- 3 Fuyu persimmons
- 1 pear—use any pear, though Asian pears are wonderful
- 1 apple—I used organic golden delicious
- 1 liter of mango juice, preferably sweetened without sugar, only with fruit juice
- 1½ cups dried cranberries
- 3 fresh-squeezed lemons, seeds removed

Step 2: Additional Spices

- ¼–½ cup sugar
- 2 tsp. sea salt
- 2 cinnamon sticks
- 3 whole cloves
- 3 whole allspice berries
- 12 or more green cardamom pods (this is a personal taste thing; I like lots of cardamom)
- 1 tsp. chopped dried whole mace pieces

Step 3: Chop Ingredients

Peel and finely chop the turmeric roots. This is tedious, and you should wear gloves because turmeric will stain your hands a nice bright yellow color for days.

Peel and chop the persimmons, pear, and apple.

Step 4: Add Ingredients to Pan and Simmer

Add all ingredients to a saucepan and simmer slowly until thickened. Avoid too much sugar. Although it is a great preservative and will make the fruit gel quicker, a slow cook has a better overall flavor.

Avoid high heat to keep the chutney from burning, becoming bitter, and/or sticking to the pan.

Step 5: Where to Find Ingredients

The majority of these items can be found at a well-stocked Indian grocery or Asian grocery, like Super H Mart. Sometimes you can find the items at Whole Foods or Central Market, but you may pay a premium.

Use over baked chicken with rice, as a side with dal or pulses, or served with cream cheese and crackers.

A strong fusion of Indian and American flavors, it has a slight crunch and a ginger/peppery taste from the turmeric.

Store in a lock-top Tupperware-type container. Keeps in the fridge for several months.

Orange, Fig, and Sage Chutney

By nonreactivepan

www.instructables.com/id/Orange-Fig-and-Sage-Chutney-1/

On a warm San Francisco Sunday we decided it was necessary to get some of our nice late-summer fruits canned up for the coming fall. The chutney I ended up with is sweet and tangy, with a nice hint of sage, which is perfect with roasts, especially pork.

It's a very simple recipe, and the way I did it required little more than measuring (sort of), chopping, and boiling down the fruits.

I hope you enjoy it.

Step 1: Ingredients

- 3 to 4 lbs oranges, sliced into 8 pieces each
- 1 basket figs (about 14 figs), sliced in half
- 3 sprigs sage, minced
- 1 lb granulated sugar
- ¼ cup lemon juice
- Rind of ½ orange

Step 2: Add Fruit and Sage

Put the oranges, figs, and sage into a large, heavy-bottomed pan, then add enough water to cover the fruit. The sage gives an earthy undertone to balance out the sweet figs and tangy oranges. I could taste it very strongly when I used the chutney for the pork roast.

Step 3: Sugar. Need I Say More?

Sugar acts as a preservative when you are making jams or other fruit-based preserves. I prefer my jam on the tart side, so I opted to reduce the sugar as much as possible. I simply pour the sugar right over the top of the fruits, and off you go.

Step 3: Add Lemon Juice

Lemon activates the natural pectin in the fruit. Pectin is what helps thicken the fruit into more of a spread or jam. You can use the plastic lemon-shaped packaged lemon juice, if it's what you have on hand. I always use that, and it tastes just fine.

Step 4: Boil It

Set over medium heat and bring to a boil. Once the mixture boils, lower the heat to a simmer and stir regularly to keep it from sticking to the pan. While you are stirring, press down on the orange pieces to release the juice. As soon as you are satisfied with the texture of your chutney (meaning it will be chunky, good for spreading on meats!), turn off the heat, making sure that your jars/lids are ready.

Step 5: Prepare Jars

Boil your jars and lids while the fruit is bubbling away in the other pan. Take a large, wide pan, fill with enough water to submerge the jars and lids, and place on the heat. Bring it to a boil.

Once the water has boiled, lower to a simmer and keep the jars in the water for five minutes.

When the chutney is ready, remove each jar and lid one by one onto a clean cloth, right side up, to keep them as sterile as possible.

Step 6: Canning

Fill your jars. Ladle chutney into each jar, filling up to the bottom of the neck of the jar, leaving headspace for the sealing to go well. Wipe down the top of the jar to make sure nothing is sticky on the outside, so that you can seal the jars and they can be opened again.

Step 7: Orange Rind

Just after you ladle the chutney into the jars, add a small amount of grated orange rind into each jar before sealing them. This adds a little fresh zing when you use the lovely finished product.

Step 8: Seal 'em Up

Put the lid on and close it as tightly as you can. Turn the jars upside down and leave to cool. This will seal the jars. Some people reboil the filled jars, but I opt not to. If you want to, this is the time to do it!

My friend, who learned to make all kinds of preserves from her grandma, said that to seal the jars you need to cool them upside down. It worked like a charm for me.

Step 9: Use It!

Once the chutney was ready to use, I made a really good pork roast that I coated in the chutney and roasted in the oven. The roast was seared on top of the stove first, then I added root veggies under the meat and coated all of it with the chutney.

Enjoy and keep on cooking!

Garlic Bread

By Jerry Chen

www.instructables.com/id/How-to-Make-Garlic-Bread/

I know you've seen plenty of recipes of how to make garlic bread, but this is my version. Hope you enjoy, and happy cooking.

Step 1: Ingredients

- French baguette bread
- Butter
- Garlic clove
- Basil
- Seasoned salt

Step 2: Cut

Cut the bread into thin, even slices.

Step 3: Butter Up

Put a slice of butter onto each slice of bread.

Step 4: Garlic Time

Get a garlic clove, peel it, and chop it into tiny pieces. Sprinkle on top of each slice of bread.

Step 5: Flavor

Sprinkle some basil and seasoned salt onto each slice.

Step 6: Bake

Bake in the oven at 400°F for 10 minutes or until golden brown.

Step 7: Done

Take out of the oven. The best part is last . . . eat it! Enjoy.

Cayenne Toasts

By Justin Tyler Tate

www.instructables.com/id/Cayenne-Toasts/

When I was a child we always had these delicious little snacks around Christmas, and now I can't even imagine Christmas without them—although you should feel free to make them any time of year. Something about the combination of spicy-sweet crunch in these makes them an addictive little snack.

Step 1: Ingredients

- 1 cup olive oil
- 2 tsp. cayenne pepper (this quantity usually gets doubled or tripled in our house)
- 1½ tsp. salt
- 1½ tsp. sugar
- ½ tsp. finely ground black pepper
- 1 tsp. paprika
- 1½ tsp. garlic powder
- 1½ tsp. onion powder
- 2 or 3 French bread loaves

Step 2: Preparation

Preheat oven to 200°F. Mix ingredients (except for the bread) and set aside. Cut the French bread into ¼-inch-thick slices. Place slices on ungreased baking sheets. Lightly coat one side of each slice with the mixture using a pastry brush, being sure to whisk the topping mixture regularly to prevent seasonings from settling. Dry in the preheated oven until crisp, about 1 hour. Remove and cool. Enjoy!

Store in airtight containers for up to two days. Cooled toasts can be packed in freezer containers and frozen for up to two months. Re-crisp frozen toasts in a preheated oven at 350°F for 5 to 7 minutes.

No-Flour Cinnamon Blueberry Pancakes

By sharlzz

www.instructables.com/id/No-Flour-Cinnamon-Blueberry-Oatmeal-Pancakes-with-/

No flour pancakes = no bloating! These pancakes are packed with vitamins, fiber, and protein—perfect for a healthy breakfast under 300 calories.

Step 1: Ingredients (makes 1 serving)

- 2 egg whites
- ⅓ cup fat-free cottage cheese (I promise, you cannot taste the cottage cheese)
- ⅓ cup oatmeal, dry
- ¼ tsp. cinnamon
- ¼ tsp. vanilla extract
- 3 tbsp. blueberries
- 2 strawberries, diced
- 2 cherries, diced
- 2 grapes, diced
- ¼ cup diced cantaloupe
- ¼ cup diced watermelon
- ⅓ peach, diced
- 8 raisins

Step 2: Directions

In a food processor, blend egg whites, cottage cheese, oatmeal, cinnamon, and vanilla extract until it resembles pancake batter, then fold in 2 tbsp. of blueberries.

Spray pan/skillet with non-stick spray and set over medium-high heat. Drop two dollops of pancake batter (about ⅓ cup each) onto the pan/skillet. Cook for 2–6 minutes on each side or until golden brown.

Place pancakes on plate and top with fruit and raisins. Voila! Two low-calorie, guilt-free, loaded with fruit pancakes. Enjoy!

Spicy Mocha Popcorn

By sylrig

www.instructables.com/id/Spicy-Mocha-Popcorn/

Sometimes it's fun to shake up the plain old butter-and-salt flavor. We've found this combination to be deep, sweet, and spicy all at once.

Step 1: Ingredients

In addition to your popcorn, you need:

- 1–2 tsp sugar
- ⅛–¼ tsp. cayenne pepper
- ¼ tsp. salt
- 1 tsp. cocoa powder
- 1 tsp. instant espresso powder

Step 2: Mix

A little goes a long way. You can tweak your proportions, but here's a start.

If you want the pepper to just peek through, use 2 tsp. sugar and ⅛ tsp. cayenne. If you want it hotter, use 1 tsp. sugar and ¼ tsp. or more of cayenne—but add in small increments, unless you have a very high tolerance for heat.

Whisk seasonings and sugar together. You should end up with about 1½ tbsp. powder.

Step 3: Sprinkle

Sprinkle this over your popped popcorn, toss, and enjoy.

Note: I make popcorn with oil on the stove. If you use a hot-air popper, you may consider drizzling oil or butter over the popcorn before adding the powder. Ditto with oil-free microwave popcorn.

Dinner

- Baked Falafel
- Chicken Pot Pie
- Chicken Tikka Masala with Turmeric Rice
- Chickpea and Carrot Tagine
- Garlic Rosemary Turkey Burgers
- Ginger Chile Chicken with Rice
- Gluten-Free Tri-Colored Ravioli with Garlic and Vegetables
- Linguine with Breadcrumbs, Garlic, Chili, and Anchovy
- Orange-Ginger-Miso Turkey with Roasted Vegetables
- Pesto Recipe with Basil, Garlic, and Pine Nuts
- Potato and Cauliflower Curry
- Risotto with Porcini, Red Wine, and Sage
- Roasted Corn and Black Bean Guacamole
- Roasted Eggplant with Garlic
- Tomato and Coconut Lentil Dhal
- Apple Sage Stuffed Acorn Squash
- Spectacular Taco Spice
- Spicy Chickpeas with Feta and Oregano

Baked Falafel

By Jessy Ellenberger

www.instructables.com/id/Baked-Falafel-Recipe/

I love falafel so very much, but I really hate frying things. The smell of oil, the mess, the flesh wounds—it's just not a good situation. Baked falafel is obviously the answer.

Step 1: Ingredients

- 15–20 oz. can chickpeas, drained or 1 cup dried chickpeas, soaked for 24 hours and drained
- ½ onion
- 6 tbsp. of chopped parsley and/or cilantro (I'm doing about ⅔ parsley, ⅓ cilantro)
- 2–3 cloves garlic, depending on your taste
- 1 tsp. cumin
- 2 tsp. coriander
- 1 tsp. chili powder
- Pinch of cayenne
- Couple tbsp. of olive oil for the falafel and for the baking sheet
- Salt and pepper to taste

It is important to note that I am using cooked chickpeas, which is fine, but if you'd like to get all traditional, simply soak a cup of dried chickpeas in the fridge for 24 hours and use those.

The falafel will be baked at 400°F for 10 minutes on the first side, 15 minutes on the second.

Step 2: Preheat and Prep

Turn the oven on to 400°F.

Roughly chop the onion, herbs, and garlic. My food processor hates big pieces. I bet yours does too, so be nice to it.

Step 3: Process

Throw everything into a food processor. You'll want to pulse it, scraping down the sides until everything is finely processed and combined, but not pureed. If you're having problems getting it to come together, add a tiny bit of olive oil to get it going.

The mixture should be slightly wet and hold together well.

Taste everything at this point and adjust seasonings as needed.

Step 4: Oil the Baking Sheet and Form Patties

I got ten patties out of the mixture. I started with balls about 2 inches wide and then flattened them. I like having them flat because they're easier to eat in a pita and they cook better in the oven. You can do bigger or smaller, but you might want to adjust the cooking time. Just play around with it.

Step 5: Cooking

After 10 minutes, take them out and carefully flip them. They'll be starting to brown and should be pretty firm.

Put them back in for 15 minutes. Once I took them out, I flipped them so you guys can see how lovely and brown they get.

The outsides should be crusty, and the insides should be nice and soft.

Step 6: Serve

Great with yogurt or sour cream, hummus, tahini sauce, guacamole, or tzatziki. I always put cucumber and red onion in mine. A little mint and tomato is good too.

Chicken Pot Pie

By jessyratfink

www.instructables.com/id/chicken-pot-pie-recipe/

Making chicken pot pie is much easier than you think, and is a good use of leftover chicken soup or a roasted chicken. Last time I made it, I used leftover chicken soup. This time I cheated and bought a rotisserie chicken and used the meat from it.

This recipe is enough for one 9–inch pot pie.

Step 1: Ingredients

- 2 tbsp. butter
- 1 carrot, diced
- 1 celery stalk, diced
- ½ onion, diced
- 1 potato, diced
- 2-3 cups chicken, cooked and diced or shredded
- Pinch of turmeric
- Pinch of poultry seasoning
- Pinch of dried thyme
- ½ cup flour
- 3 cups chicken broth
- salt and pepper
- Pie crust of choice (I used a ready–made crust for this one, but it is really, really good with a bacon fat pie crust.)
- You can also add frozen corn and peas to it

As far as a container to bake the pie in, you'll want a deep ceramic or glass pie plate.

Step 2: Sautéing and Adding Seasonings

Add a couple tablespoons of butter to a pan over medium heat. Add in the carrot, celery, onion and potatoes. Cook, stirring frequently, for about five minutes until the vegetables start to soften. Add in the chicken and seasonings. (Please note I added way too much turmeric by accident. When I say a pinch, I mean a teeny amount—no more than ¼ teaspoon.)

Stir around and cook for another couple minutes.

Preheat the oven to 375°F.

Step 3: Add the Flour and Stock

Pour in the flour and stir it around so it coats everything. Let this cook for a couple minutes, stirring it the entire time.

Now, pour in the stock and stir really well. Break up any flour clumps you see and let the mixture come to a bubble. This will help thicken it.

At this point, taste the sauce and add some extra seasoning or salt and pepper if necessary. Turn off the heat.

Step 4: Baking

Pour the chicken mix into a pie pan and cover with your crust. Seal the edges of the crust by pressing them onto the edges of the pan.

Cut slits in the top to help release the steam that will occur during cooking.

Put the pie pan on a baking sheet and pop it into a 375°F oven. Cook for 25–30 minutes or until the crust is nicely browned.

See the bottom photo? That is why we're putting the pie on a baking sheet. Filling explosion!

Chicken Tikka Masala with Turmeric Rice

By Nerdinista

www.instructables.com/id/Chicken-Tikka-Masala-with-Turmeric-Rice/

Step 1: Chicken Tikka Masala

Ingredients:

- 2 chicken breasts
- ½ large onion
- 1 medium tomato
- 2 small cloves garlic
- ¼ piece (about 1 inch) ginger root
- 1 tbsp. canola oil
- 1 tsp. cumin
- 1 tsp. garam masala
- 1 tsp. salt
- 2 tbsp. sugar
- 3 tbsp. water
- 1 tbsp. olive oil

For the marinade:

- ⅓ tsp. salt
- 1 tsp. garam masala
- 2 small cloves garlic
- ¼ piece ginger
- 2 tbsp. plain (or vanilla) yogurt

Trim chicken and cut into small cubes. Mix all marinade ingredients and fold into chicken. Marinate at least 15 minutes, but the longer the better.

Chop onion, tomato, garlic, and ginger. Sauté onions in canola oil over low heat until golden brown. Add garlic and ginger and sauté until fragrant. Add tomatoes and sauté until moisture has evaporated. Add cumin, garam masala, salt, and sugar, then simmer 2 minutes. Add water and simmer 2 more minutes.

In a separate pan, heat olive oil and sauté chicken over low heat. Add chicken to sauce and mix well. Bring briefly to a boil before removing from heat. Transfer to plate and serve!

Step 2: Turmeric Rice

Ingredients:

- 1 cup rice (I use basic brown)
- ½ tsp. salt
- ½ tsp. turmeric
- 1 tbsp. butter
- 1 cup chicken broth

Wash and drain rice—soak in fresh water for 20 minutes and drain. Melt butter in pan on low, add rice, and stir fry for 1 minute. Add salt and turmeric, then stir. Add chicken broth and bring to a boil. Reduce heat, cover, and let simmer for 15 minutes. Remove from heat and let steam for 5 minutes. Stir and serve!

Chickpea and Carrot Tagine

By jessyratfink

www.instructables.com/id/Chickpea-and-carrot-tangine/

This is a quick and easy vegan meal for nights when you want something fast. It's also something I make when I get to the end of my groceries, as I always have these ingredients on hand.

Step 1: Ingredients

- 1 small onion, diced (or half a large one)
- 14.5-oz can chickpeas, drained
- 2 carrots, cut into slices
- 2–3 cloves garlic, minced
- ½ tsp. cumin
- ½ tsp. turmeric
- Good pinch cinnamon
- Good pinch cayenne
- Salt and pepper to taste
- 1 cup water

This is best served over rice, so you'll also need:

- 1 cup rice (any kind you like)
- 1¾ cups water
- Salt

Step 2: Cook the Veggies

Put a little olive oil in your pan over medium heat and dump in the veggies. Let them cook for a few minutes, or until the onions get translucent and the carrots begin to soften.

Step 3: Add the Spices, Chickpeas, and Garlic

Stir it together very well and let it cook for a couple minutes. You just want the spices and garlic to get really fragrant, then you'll know you're ready!

Step 4: Add Water and Simmer

Add the water and mix, and let it come to a boil. Then turn down heat to a simmer and cover the pan. You'll let this cook for about 20 minutes, covered.

Step 5: Make the Rice

While it simmers, you'll have just enough time to make the rice.

I always do 1 cup of rice and 1¾ cups of water. Bring the cup of water to a boil with a generous pinch of salt, pour in the rice, turn the heat to low, and cover. Cook for 18 minutes, then turn off the heat and let it sit, covered, for an additional 10 minutes, and then fluff with a fork.

I don't use any butter or oil, but feel free to add some if you'd like.

Step 6: Check the Liquid Level and Serve

After 20 minutes, the liquid should have reduced quite a bit. If not, turn up the heat and let it simmer uncovered for a few minutes while your rice finishes getting nice and fluffy. You still want it to be slightly runny, but not a soup. (The liquid is excellent once it soaks into the rice!)

This is also a good time to check the seasonings and add more as desired!

Spoon it over rice and eat! Cilantro and parsley are good with this, as is sriracha.

Garlic Rosemary Turkey Burgers

By ewilhelm

www.instructables.com/id/Garlic-Rosemary-Turkey-Burgers/

This is a fragrant alternative to the boring hamburger. It's easy to freeze for later, too.

Step 1: Ingredients

- Garlic
- Rosemary
- Dried mustard
- Ground black pepper
- Ground turkey
- Tomatoes, lettuce, onions and/or other ingredients for garnish

Step 2: Grate Fresh Garlic

Step 3: Finely Chop Fresh Rosemary

Step 4: Add Dried Mustard and Ground Black Pepper

Step 5: Add Turkey

Squish together with ground turkey to mix. Detach small blobs for patty formation.

Step 6: Make Patties

Make nice, big, flat patties and pile onto a plate.

Step 7: Grill

Grill until nicely browned. Check interior with a sharp knife to make sure it bleeds (not pink).

Step 8: Garnish

Garnish in appropriate yuppie fashion.

Step 9: Freeze Extras

Freeze extras between sheets of waxed paper. Stack them in pairs overnight, then transfer to plastic freezer bags for longer-term storage.

Ginger Chile Chicken with Rice

By garnishrecipes

www.instructables.com/id/Ginger-Chile-Chicken-With-Rice/

Poached chicken in an aromatic broth with chile and shaved ginger—this meal is light, refreshing, and filling. The fluffy rice is simmered in the ginger and onion broth, which is prepared with pan juices from the quickly poached chicken.

Would you believe me if I told you this meal came from some sauce packets left over from dim sum, discounted frozen chicken, and the bottom of the rice bag? It's amazing what you can whip out of your refrigerator at 6:00 p.m. when the entire house is hungry.

This is bachelor chow at its finest. I hope you enjoy it as much as we did. It's an excellent short-notice save. I was browsing recipes on my phone shortly before cooking and came across what looked like a goodie, but I had about half the ingredients.

The concept for the dish was inspired by this photo of a *New York Times* recipe for Hainanese Chicken with Rice.

Step 1: Ingredients

Serves two, generously.

- 12 oz. of barely defrosted chicken
- 2 stalks of lemongrass, (optional)
- 2-inch piece of ginger
- 1 onion
- 4 cups of water
- 2 cups of uncooked rice
- Take-out packets of chile paste and soy

To prepare the ingredients, defrost the chicken briefly (one minute in the microwave on high). The chicken needs to be slightly frozen in order for it to poach quickly.

If using, cut the lemongrass stalk into 3-inch segments, discarding the green leaves. Add the lemongrass to a quart-size measuring cup with water. Soak until needed.

Peel the ginger. Very carefully shave it with a vegetable peeler or use a knife to cut it into paper-thin slices.

Slice the onion in half. Peel off the exterior, slice off the ends, and cut it into thin half-moons about ½-inch thick.

Step 2: Poach the Chicken

Generously salt the chicken. The salt creates a surface between the chicken and the pan until the chicken defrosts more.

Heat a large saucepan to medium-high and add the chicken. Cover immediately. As the steam melts the frozen chicken, the chicken will take on a poached texture.

Set your timer for 10 minutes. When the timer goes off, lift the chicken onto another plate, but reserve the cooking juices.

Step 3: Make the Onion Ginger Broth

Add the lemongrass stalks, ginger, onion, and water to the pan. Cover and simmer for about 5 minutes, until you can smell the aromatics. When your kitchen smells heavily of ginger, you'll know it's time to add the rice.

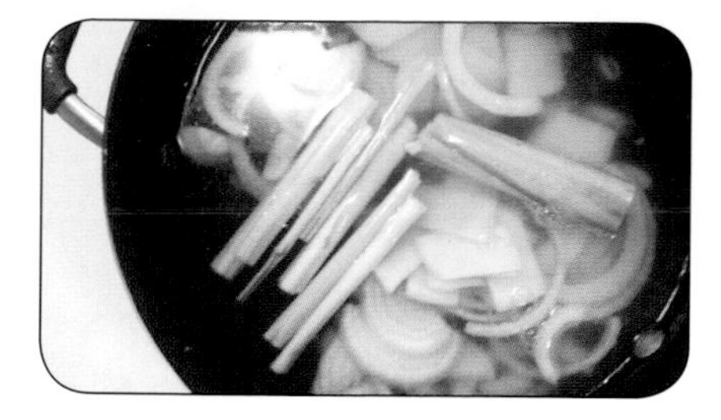

Step 4: Simmer the Rice in the Broth

Remove the lemongrass and discard (or save for additional use). Dish the ginger and onion onto the plate holding the poached chicken. Add the rice, cover, and turn the heat up to medium. Trust me—with the amount of simmering happening, the broth will have reduced and will soak into the rice.

Set a timer for 20 minutes. Leave the heat on medium.

Step 5: Assemble the Rice Bowl

When the rice has almost completely absorbed the broth (think moist, not dripping), dish the rice into the bottom of a bowl. The rice will taste like the broth it cooked in; a little extra moisture is just fine with this dish.

Split the chicken and onion portions, and add a serving to each bowl.

Garnish with a little chile paste and soy over the top. A great take-out twist is soy vinegar and chile-garlic paste. Sriracha and soy sauce work just as well.

Gluten-Free Tri-Colored Ravioli with Garlic and Vegetables

By ectadie

www.instructables.com/id/Gluten-Free-Tri-Colored-Ravioli-with-Roasted-Butte/

I decided I wanted to make a ravioli main course. Since I already had leftover gluten-free flours I decided to go gluten-free.

Although this recipe has a decent number of steps, I promise none of them are very difficult. Also, there are tons of steps along the way that you can vary in this recipe to make it exactly what you like. Don't have a gluten allergy? You can just use a regular flour pasta recipe! Prefer other fillings? No problem!

I tried to make up the simplest possible gluten-free pasta recipe—the most expensive ingredient was the xanthan gum, but I only needed a little bit, so I know it will last me a long time.

Step 1: Ingredients

For pasta:

- 2 oz. spinach for green pasta
- ½ cup tapioca flour
- ½ cup cornstarch
- 3 tbsp. potato starch
- ¾ tsp. salt
- 4½ tsp. xanthan gum
- 3 large eggs
- 2 tbsp. vegetable oil
- 1 tbsp. beet powder for red pasta (I stumbled across this in the bulk section of Whole Foods).

For filling:

- 1 cup of chickpeas, either cooked or from a can (I give instructions for cooking them on the next step in case you want to do that)
- 1 cup butternut squash
- 2 cloves garlic
- ½ white onion
- 1 tsp. olive oil
- salt and pepper to taste
- ⅔ cup ricotta cheese
- ⅓ cup Parmesan cheese
- 1 tsp. sage, chopped
- Juice from ½ lemon

For sage-infused butter sauce:

- 4 tbsp. butter
- 5 large sage leaves
- Salt and pepper
- Lemon juice (optional)

Step 2: Soak/Boil Chickpeas (optional)

This step needs to be started a day in advance. The night before you want to make your ravioli, rinse the chickpeas in cold water, place in a bowl, and fill the bowl with water. Let this sit at room temperature overnight, for at least 8 hours.

The next day, drain water from the bowl, place the chickpeas in a pot, and fill the pot with cool water. Turn the heat to high on your stove, bring the water to a boil, and then reduce heat to a simmer with a cover on your pan. Simmer the chickpeas for about 3 hours, or until they are soft. Drain the chickpeas, salt them to taste, and set them aside.

Note: I think this tastes the best, but for simplicity's sake you could definitely just use a can of chickpeas. Then, you just open the can and they are ready to go. Just be careful if there is any salt added.

Step 3: Roasted Garlic

Put two peeled garlic cloves on a sheet of aluminum foil about 5 inches long. Add about a ¼ tsp. of olive oil and spread it over the garlic. Wrap the garlic up tightly in the foil. Add another layer of foil on top if you want to be extra careful. Place the wrapped garlic on a foil-lined baking sheet. Wait until the next step to put the garlic in the oven—it will be done at the same time as the butternut squash.

Step 4: Roasted Butternut Squash

Preheat oven to 400°F. Cut the squash into 1½-inch cubes. Place on foil-lined pan with the garlic and spray with non-stick spray. Salt generously. Place pan in oven and bake until a fork can be easily inserted into the tender squash. At this point, your kitchen will smell amazing!

Step 5: Caramelized Onion

While your garlic and butternut squash are roasting, dice half a white onion. Put it in a pan with about a teaspoon of olive oil. Turn to high heat for a few minutes, stirring constantly. After the onion has heated up, reduce heat to low, and let them cook slowly until they are a deep caramel color. Salt and pepper to taste.

Step 6: Blend Squash, Onion, and Garlic to Make Filling

Place about a cup of butternut squash into a food processor. (Set aside the rest to snack on!) Add the onion and garlic and pulse until mashed up and well mixed. If you want your ravioli filling to have a super smooth consistency, pulse the mixture more.

Next, add your ricotta and parmesan cheeses, chopped sage, and lemon juice. Adjust seasonings with salt, pepper, sage, or anything else you like. (Chili pepper flakes might be good!) Mix well.

Note: Everything up until this step can be prepared the night before you actually want to make your ravioli.

Step 7: Prepare Pasta

Sauté spinach in a pan and then pulse in a food processor until broken up and mushy.

Combine the tapioca flour, cornstarch, potato starch, salt, and xanthan gum Make a well in the center and add in eggs and oil. Scramble eggs with oil in the bowl, slowly incorporating more and more of the dry ingredients.

Separate out about ⅓ of the dough. Split this smaller amount into two balls of dough and place into separate bowls. To one bowl add the beet powder and mix well. To the other bowl add the spinach and mix well. Leave the larger amount of dough without any added color.

Knead each pile of dough separately for a few minutes. If they get too tough, let them rest for about 10–15 minutes while covered with plastic wrap.

Step 8: Roll Pasta Dough

Roll out each pasta dough separately, using tapioca flour to flour your surface. Make each dough thin enough that when lifted towards light, it is slightly transparent. For ravioli, the thinner you can get your pasta dough the better! If you kneaded and floured the dough well with tapioca flour, this shouldn't be too difficult.

Add color stripes: Cut thin, long strips of red and green dough and place them on top of the plain dough. Spread a thin layer of water over the top where you want to lay your strips, to act like glue to hold the two dough pieces together. Next, roll out your dough so it's thin again.

Step 9: Make Ravioli

Cut out ravioli into any shapes you want. I just went with squares because they're easy! Since your dough is only striped on one side, be sure to keep the pretty side facing out of your ravioli.

Add a small dollop of filling onto a square of dough. Using your finger, put a small amount of water along the clean edges of the pasta to act like glue for the top layer. Lay another piece of pasta on top and press firmly to seal. Try to push any air out of the center of the ravioli to avoid having the pasta open up while boiling later.

Step 10: Cook Ravioli and Make Sage-Infused Butter Sauce

Boil water in a pot over high heat. Cook ravioli in boiling water for about 3 minutes, until they float to the top.

While the ravioli are cooking, melt the butter in a pan and add sage leaves. Let the butter and sage cook together until the butter browns slightly. Salt and pepper to taste, and add lemon juice here if you would like.

When ravioli are finished boiling, drain the water and add the ravioli to the pan with the hot butter. Brown them just a tiny bit.

Serve immediately and enjoy!

Linguine with Breadcrumbs, Garlic, Chili, and Anchovy

By Tessa Augustyniak

www.instructables.com/id/linguine-with-breadcrumbs-garlic-chilli-and-anch/

I love this recipe, and there are so many possible variations. I almost always have the ingredients for this in the house, so it's a great meal when you haven't got much in the house or are pushed for time. Even if you think you don't like anchovies I urge you to try this recipe. They disappear into the sauce to give a rich and salty flavor to the whole dish. But if you really can't bring yourself to use them, leave them out, but add some extra olive oil to help the sauce along, or try a sun-dried tomato paste instead.

Check out more of my projects on my site: http://eating-properly.blogspot.com/

Step 1: Ingredients

- 70 g fresh bread crumbs
- 1 tbsp. olive oil
- ½ tsp. fennel seeds
- 250 g linguine or spaghetti
- 50 g tin anchovy fillets in olive oil
- 4 garlic cloves, finely chopped
- ½–1 tsp. chili flakes
- Freshly ground black pepper
- Handful of flat leaf parsley

Step 2: Prepare Breadcrumbs

Heat a cast iron skillet or thick-based frying pan and toast the bread crumbs in the olive oil until golden brown. Just before you remove from the heat add in the fennel seeds and lightly toast. Put the crumbs into a dish and set to one side.

Step 3: Cook the Pasta

Cook the linguine according to the package instructions in well-salted water.

Step 4: Start the Sauce

About 5 minutes before the pasta is cooked, heat a wide frying pan over medium-high heat.

Carefully pour in the oil from the anchovy tin and cook the garlic and chili flakes until golden.

Step 5: Add Anchovies

Next add the anchovy fillets and, using a wooden spoon, squish them until they have broken down into the garlic and chili mix. Add a couple ladles of the water used to cook the pasta to help this along so that you end up with a creamy puree.

Step 6: Finish the Sauce

Once the pasta is cooked, add it to the anchovy mixture, followed by the black pepper and parsley.

Step 7: Finish and Serve

Finally, add the breadcrumbs and stir through. Serve and enjoy!

Orange-Ginger-Miso Turkey with Roasted Vegetables

By canida

www.instructables.com/id/Orange-Ginger-Miso-Turkey-with-Roasted-Vegetables/

Give even a standard supermarket turkey an extra kick of flavor.

Step 1: Make Miso Paste

Ingredients:

- 2–4 large scoops miso paste
- Grated ginger
- Grated garlic
- Sesame oil
- Orange zest
- Dash soy sauce

Combine all ingredients to make a soft paste. Taste it and adjust seasonings—this will flavor your bird, so make sure it's to your liking.

Step 2: Find a Turkey and a Pan

Get yourself a nice turkey and a pan with plenty of room for it to sit. I've got a very small (8 lb.) turkey and a rather large pan that can accommodate a much larger bird. Yours can fit more snugly.

There are many varieties of turkey to choose from. The standard production turkey is a Broad Breasted White, which has such a large breast that mating is impossible, and all birds are the product of artificial insemination. There are also heritage breeds of turkey, such as the Bourbon Red, Bronze, and Narragansett, which have smaller breasts but generally more flavorful meat. Any of these can be raised free-range, which usually results in lower fat content, more dark meat, and larger/stronger bones. These features usually cost more, unfortunately.

Step 3: Rub and Stuff

Rub the miso paste under the turkey's skin. Stuff orange slices and onions under the skin as well. Place the turkey in the pan and surround it with chopped onions, root vegetables (carrots, regular or sweet potatoes, celery root, parsnips, etc), tomatoes, parsley, and pepper. If you're using a low-fat bird (heritage or true free-range turkey) then drizzle the veggies with olive oil and stir to coat. This will prevent them from sticking and burning. A regular production turkey will drop plenty of liquid.

Step 4: Roast

Roast the bird in a 400°F oven for the first 30 minutes, then turn the heat down to 350°F and cook until an instant-read thermometer reads about 165°F at the thickest part of the breast and thigh. Rotate the pan periodically during cooking to ensure even heating. If the breast gets too dark or hits 165°F before the thigh, tent the breast with foil and continue cooking. The 180°F quoted by the turkey companies is bogus tail covering—it's like cooking the bird to super-dry-extra-crispy-well-done. The turkey will be dry and overcooked, but hey, any potential pathogens are dead! (Salmonella dies at 160°F.)

Step 5: Carve and Serve

After you've impressed everyone with your gorgeous roasted bird, let it sit for a while so it can cool and redistribute juices. Remove all the roasted vegetables to a serving bowl, drain and reserve juices for use in gravy, then carve the turkey. Find a big cutting board and a nice, sharp knife.

First remove the legs/thighs. Cut through the skin connecting them to the breast and wiggle the leg to expose the hip joint. Cut through the surrounding flesh to make things clearer, wiggle the leg/thigh again, and cut through the joint. This should be easy if you work your knife into the gap properly—no bones involved.

Perform a similar operation to remove the wings from the body, separate the leg/thigh joint, and separate the wings into individual segments.

If any portions (most likely the thighs) seem undercooked, return them to the oven separately for a quick trip under the broiler. Now you've got a round lump of predominantly breast meat still attached to the bird. Stabilize the body with a long fork and trim off slices of the breast until you reach the underlying bone. Alternatively, use your fingers to separate both sides of the breast from the carcass in separate chunks, then slice the breast directly on the cutting board. This technique allows for better slicing, and in any direction. Place the turkey in an large bowl or on a platter and serve warm. If it must wait, cover the dish with foil and warm it in the oven briefly before moving it to the table.

Pesto Recipe with Basil, Garlic, and Pine Nuts

By canida
www.instructables.com/id/Pesto-2/

Pesto is the perfect green food. Serve it on pasta, with eggs, with cheese, on crackers, with chicken or fish, worked into pasta or tortillas, or with just about anything else that needs fantastic flavor. I recently ate some marinated artichoke hearts that had been tossed in pesto—they were excellent.

Step 1: Ingredients

- Italian basil
- Several garlic cloves
- Pine nuts
- Extra virgin olive oil
- Parmesan cheese
- Salt

Step 2: Basil and Garlic

Collect a large amount of Italian basil from your favorite farmers' market or supermarket. (Don't use Thai basil, as the flavor is strong enough to be bitter in pesto.) Wash and destem basil, then pat dry with a kitchen towel. Pulse several cloves of garlic in the food processer, then add handfuls of basil until everything is chopped. The bowl will be a nice emerald-green color.

Step 3: Toast Pine Nuts

Toast a pan full of pine nuts over low heat, stirring occasionally to prevent burning. They will smell nicely nutty when done. Take them off the heat before they reach the desired toastiness, as they'll continue cooking for a while afterwards.

Step 4: Add Other Ingredients

The traditional version:

Add pine nuts, extra virgin olive oil, Parmesan cheese, and salt to taste. The olive oil controls the consistency—add more for a softer blend. More parmesan makes it more crumbly.

For freezing:

If you plan to freeze your pesto, don't add the cheese! It doesn't take freeze/thaws well, and is easy to add after you've defrosted the pesto. You can add lemon juice to prevent oxidation.

Freakish (but tasty) variations:

If the basil turns out to be slightly bitter, you can add some honey or agave nectar. Salt, pepper, chili powder, and Worchestershire sauce are frequent additions. Taste to see what you like. If you're trying to make vegan pesto by skipping the cheese, add more salt and up the nuts and weird flavorings to make up for the taste, as Parmesan is pretty strong!

You can make all sorts of wacky versions—forget tradition, figure out what tastes good to you and create something new.

Step 5: Finished

When you've added everything, the pesto should look something like the photo. If you add parmesan cheese, it will be lighter in color. Now dump your pesto on pasta, spread it on bread and cover it with tomatoes, or make a pesto egg crepe.

Step 6: Freezing Instructions

I fill ramekins with the pesto, wrap them in Saran wrap, label with the date, and freeze. Don't freeze it with the cheese; it's much better to freeze without, then add cheese after thawing.

Potato and Cauliflower Curry

By jessyratfink

www.instructables.com/id/Potato-and-cauliflower-curry/

This curry is a super easy and delicious meal if you've got a well-stocked spice cabinet! The main ingredients in this curry are cauliflower and potatoes, but you can easily add some meat or additional veggies if you'd like!

I suppose this recipe is more of a course in winging it instead of set rules. I normally make up this recipe as I go along, but here I tried to measure things out for once.

And best of all, you can be eating in an hour!

Step 1: Ingredients:

- 1 small cauliflower
- 2-4 potatoes (you want the amount of potatoes to be equal to the amount of cauliflower)
- 1 onion
- 2 small tomatoes
- 3-4 garlic cloves
- 2-inch ginger root
- Jalapeño or other spicy pepper, optional
- 1 tbsp. curry powder
- ½ tsp. cumin
- ½ tsp. cumin seeds
- ½ tsp. turmeric
- ½ tsp. coriander
- ½ tsp. chili powder
- Salt
- 1½ cups water or veggie/chicken stock if you're feeling fancy
- Handful of cilantro

The cumin seeds are entirely optional, but I think it gives it a great taste. I love biting into one! I prefer red potatoes with the skin on for this recipe. And, of course, feel free to leave the cilantro out if you hate it.

Please note that the spices are just good base amounts for the recipe—you can add even more if you like! More cumin seeds and chili powder always make a good curry.

You're also going to need a big pot to cook this in. The flatter it can all get, the better it will cook.

Step 2: Prep the Veggies

Remove the stem from the cauliflower and chop it into small pieces, then chop up the potatoes, and dice the onion and tomatoes.

Mince the garlic and ginger, then chop the jalapeño or other pepper as finely as you like, if you're using it.

Get a large pan with about a tablespoon of oil in it heating up over medium heat.

Step 3: Sautéing

Once the oil is hot, dump in the onions and hot pepper and cook until softened. Then add in the garlic and ginger and cook until fragrant. At this point, add all of your spices along with a good pinch of salt. Stir this around until everything is nice and coated.

Step 4: Simmering

Add the potatoes, cauliflower, and tomato to the pot and stir everything together. You want everything to get pretty orange at this point.

Once everything is coated in oil and spices, add 1½ cups water or stock and stir again. (Note that if you added meat or additional veggies, you will need more liquid! I like the liquid level to be about ½-inch below the veggies.) Now cover the pan, drop it down to a simmer, and let it cook for 15 minutes.

Once the 15 minutes are up, check for seasonings! I'll normally add a little more curry powder at this point, and maybe a little more salt. It is good to ease into both things.

If it's not spicy enough, add more chili powder or cayenne. If you'd like a little more acid, put in extra coriander—it's very citrusy. Taste too sweet for you? Add a little turmeric.

Once everything tastes right to you, cover the pot and simmer for an additional 15 minutes minimum! If you have longer to simmer it, it'll be thicker and taste a little stronger. It's up to you.

Step 5: Serve

Once it's cooked long enough for you, take it off the heat and chop up a handful of cilantro and mix that in.

It's super yummy with pickled red onions or spicy onion chutney or relish. Anything with a little vinegar or acid is a great friend of this curry—even hot sauces!

This recipe is also good with naan or over a bowl of rice. Or just by itself!

And any leftovers you have will taste even better.

Risotto with Porcini, Red Wine, and Sage

By nonreactivepan

www.instructables.com/id/Risotto-with-Porcini-Red-Wine-and-Sage/

Fall-like weather always makes me want to have warm, satisfying rice or pasta dishes. The other day I decided to break out my stand-by risotto recipe. It's fairly simple and oh so satisfying.

Just a note, I don't eat cheese, so the only dairy product in this recipe is butter: I can't seem to remove it completely from my repertoire. There's just no replacement for the flavor and creaminess butter brings to rice. If you'd like to make this completely vegan, replace the butter with olive oil, as it works just fine.

Step 1: Ingredients

- 4 bouillon cubes (I use porcini cubes, but use whatever type you like)
- 4 cups water
- 1 cup red wine (or enough to fully cover the mushrooms)
- 1 bag dried porcini mushrooms
- 3 tbsp. butter
- 2 tbsp. olive oil
- 3 cloves garlic, minced
- 2 cups arborio rice
- 4 fresh sage leaves, minced (or ¼ tsp. dried sage)
- salt, pepper, and red pepper to taste

Step 2: Make the Stock

Heat the bouillon and the water in a large saucepan. Bring to a boil, making sure all the cubes dissolve completely. Lower to a simmer and stir occasionally until it is time to add the liquid to the rice.

Step 3: Soak the Dried Porcini

Pour the cup of red wine into a small saucepan. Add the porcini mushrooms, making sure there is enough wine to completely submerge them. Bring the wine to a boil, then reduce to a simmer. Keep simmering for about 15 minutes, until the mushrooms are soft. Pour the wine and mushrooms through a sieve or strainer, making sure to capture all of the liquid in a bowl beneath the strainer. Chop mushrooms coarsely and set aside.

Step 4: Start the Rice

Heat a large, heavy-bottomed pot over medium heat. Add butter and allow to melt, then add the olive oil. Lower heat to medium-low and add the minced garlic. Sauté the garlic until almost opaque. Add rice, stirring to cover all the grains in the butter/oil mixture.

Quite simply, you are trying to get the rice to cook slowly so that it will toast somewhat in the beginning and then take its time absorbing all of the lovely stock and wine you are going to add to it. Take your time here, and if it seems things are starting to stick or burn, lower the heat and relax. If you'd like a glass of wine, now's a good time to grab one, as you get ready to stir for a bit.

Step 5: Cook the Rice

Add ½ cup of the stock to the rice pot, stirring constantly. As soon as the stock has been completely absorbed, add another ½ cup and stir until absorbed. Alternating ½ cups of stock and wine, continue adding liquid and stirring to absorb until all the liquid has been added. The rice should be soft and ready to eat once all the liquid has been incorporated. Remove the pot from the heat and add the sage, salt, pepper, and red pepper flakes to the rice.

This is the most time-consuming step, but again, just take it slow and don't worry, you'll be eating soon enough. Make sure that all of the liquid gets absorbed before you make a move to add more. It's tough to wait. I know I've rushed it before and regretted it after the fact. The rice needs time to soak it all up before it takes another breath and is ready to drink up some more.

It'll be well worth your effort (and the number of pans you'll have to clean). It's a great fall dish, especially if you live somewhere where the weather has actually started to shift to coolness.

Enjoy and eat up!

Roasted Corn and Black Bean Guacamole

By garnishrecipes

www.instructables.com/id/Roasted-Corn-and-Black-Bean-Guacamole/

For your next barbecue or potluck, try a sweet and spicy mix-up to traditional guacamole with roasted corn and black bean guacamole. Roasted corn adds a fresh-off-the-grill flavor, and black beans pack protein into the dish. The cayenne-lime marinade gives the recipe an extra boost. This recipe serves eight.

Step 1: Ingredients

- 1 lb. corn, roasted (Roasted corn is available in the frozen section at Trader Joe's supermarkets)
- 15 oz. black beans, drained
- 1 green bell pepper, minced
- 3 large avocados, diced
- 2 limes, juiced
- ½ cup olive oil
- 2 tbsp. sugar
- 1½ tsp. sea salt
- 1 tsp. cayenne pepper
- ½ tsp. black pepper

Step 2: Instructions

Roast the corn on the grill then cut the corn along each side. Add the corn into a large bowl.

Drain the black beans and rinse. Add to the large bowl.

Cut the green bell pepper in half and pull out the stem. Cut into small strips and cut again crosswise into fine cubes. Add to the large bowl.

Cut the avocado in half and remove the pit by carefully inserting a knife into the pit and twisting the knife. Divide each half into cubes and scoop out the cubes using a large spoon. Add to the large bowl.

In a small bowl, mix together the olive oil, lime juice, sugar, sea salt, cayenne, and black pepper. Pour the spice marinade into the large bowl and stir thoroughly. Done!

Roasted Eggplant with Garlic

By canida

www.instructables.com/id/Roasted-Eggplant-with-Garlic/

This is a great way to cook eggplant with minimal prep time.

Step 1: Ingredients

- Chinese or Japanese eggplant
- Garlic, chopped
- Olive Oil
- Black Pepper
- Cajun Spice and/or salt
- Scallions, parsley, chili powder, cumin, oregano, rosemary (optional)

Step 2: Prepare Eggplant

Find some nice Chinese or Japanese eggplant. These are the long, skinny varieties, easily distinguishable from the globular Italian eggplant. Do not attempt to use Italian eggplant for this dish—the skin is too thick, and the flesh isn't as sweet. Wash the eggplant, trim off the caps, halve lengthwise, and place halves in a greased baking dish. I generally use spray canola oil and give the cut surfaces of the eggplant another spray to keep them moist during baking.

Step 3: Season

Chop a big pile of garlic, or use a jar of the pre-chopped stuff. Garlic salt really won't cut it. Sprinkle the chopped garlic over the eggplant to your preferred density, then drizzle the eggplant with a bit of olive oil. Grind fresh pepper over the top and sprinkle with cajun spice and/or a bit of salt.

Optional additions: scallions, parsley, and so on can be chopped in with the garlic, chili powder, cumin, oregano, rosemary, or spice/herb of your choice to sprinkle on top.

Step 4: Roast

Put the pan in a 350°F oven for about 30–45 minutes. The eggplant will thin and curl on itself a bit, and the garlic will become a crisp and nutty brown on top. At this point, you can remove the eggplant and eat it directly, but I prefer to shut off the oven and let it slowly cool. This extra hour sitting at a low temperature dries the eggplant out a bit more, concentrating and mellowing the flavors.

Step 5: Serve

You can serve these warm or at room temperature; it's all good. They make great appetizers when cut into segments and served at room temperature, and, of course, they make a lovely vegetarian side dish for those family gatherings.

Tomato and Coconut Lentil Dhal

By chipbuttiesandnoodlesoup
www.instructables.com/id/tomato-and-coconut-lentil-dhal/

This is a healthy, comforting dish that you just know is doing you good when you eat it. Flavored with immunity-boosting ginger, garlic, and chili, this curry is great for a cold winter evening. It is inspired by an Indian dhal (also spelt dal, daal, dahl), a lentil stew that is a staple of the Indian diet. This is a great vegetarian main dish because it is packed with protein.

I love curries and chili and get a bit distracted if I don't get my daily chili fix in at least one of my meals. I have heard there is such a thing as chili addiction. You can obviously add more or less chilis depending on their strength and your preference.

Preparation time: 10 minutes

Cooking time: 1 hour

Serves 2 as main dish or 4 as a side dish

Step 1: Ingredients

- 1 cup green (puy) lentils (or lentil of choice, but remember to follow your packet's cooking instructions as it may be different from mine)
- 1 tsp. turmeric
- 1 tbsp. oil
- 1 onion, chopped
- 1 tsp. fennel seed
- 1 tsp. coriander seed
- 1 tsp. mustard seed
- 1 bay leaf
- 1 inch ginger root grated
- 4-5 garlic cloves, crushed
- 4-5 chilis
- 1 tin chopped tomatoes
- 3 tbsp. dessicated coconut
- 1 liter boiling water or vegetable stock
- Salt and pepper

Step 2: Prepare the lentils, onions and spices

Wash lentils thoroughly in cold water then add to a pan with cold water and the turmeric and boil uncovered for 15 minutes.

While this is happening, add the oil to another pan and, when hot, add the chopped onion. Sauté until golden brown and caramelized.

When the onions are browned add the spice seeds and bay leaf and sauté for a few minutes to release the flavor.

Step 3: Add the Remaining Ingredients and Simmer Until Soft

Add the ginger, garlic, and chilis and continue to sauté for a few minutes before adding the tomatoes and dessicated coconut. Stir this together and top up with about 1 liter of boiling water or stock. Simmer for about an hour, until the lentils are soft.

Step 4: Add Salt and Pepper

Add salt and pepper to taste. Now serve with rice, flat bread, or potatoes. I served this with simple boiled white rice and my za'atar roast potatoes.

Apple Sage Stuffed Acorn Squash

By Meg Brock

www.instructables.com/id/Stuffed-Acorn-Squash-gluten-free/

This is the perfect dish to make when the weather starts to get cool and perfectly ripe acorn squash begin to appear at the grocery store. The combination of sage, apples, and squash works really well together and is very filling!

Step 1: Ingredients

- 1 large acorn squash
- 1 large apple, chopped into ½-inch pieces (peeling is optional; I am lazy and leave the skin on)
- 1 large white onion, peeled and chopped into ½-inch pieces
- 1 lb ground beef
- ¼ cup brown sugar
- 1 tsp. dried sage
- ¼ tsp. salt
- ¼ tsp. pepper
- 2 tsp. coconut flour

Step 2: Instructions

Preheat your oven to 375°F. Wash and dry the squash. Using a large, sharp knife, cut the squash in half vertically. Using a spoon, scoop out all of the seeds and throw them in the trash.

Place the two halves of acorn squash cut-side down in a large baking dish (I use glass Pyrex) and bake for 40 minutes.

While the squash is baking, heat a large saucepan over medium-high heat. Add your chopped apple and onion to the pan and cook, stirring frequently, for 4 minutes. Add the ground beef and break up with a spoon. Cook for another 5 minutes,

stirring frequently. Add in your brown sugar, sage, salt, and pepper. Cook for one more minute, stirring until everything is well mixed.

Remove the pan from heat and stir in the coconut flour. This helps all the juices at the bottom of the pan to absorb into your stuffing mixture.

When the squash are done cooking, remove the baking dish from the oven (but leave oven turned on) and flip the squash right-side up so that they form little bowls. Spoon your beef mixture into each squash. Depending on how big your squash is, you might have leftover beef mixture, which you can cook in a ramekin and eat as leftovers the next day.

Return the baking dish to the oven and bake for another 20 minutes. Cool 5 minutes before serving because these are VERY hot and will burn your mouth if eaten right out of the oven.

Makes 2 servings (plus leftovers) or 3–4 smaller servings if you use 2 small acorn squash.

Notes: I like having acorn squash on my counter because they will sit there and last for weeks without going bad! This is a very easy dinner to make when you have nothing left in the fridge. I always have ground beef in my freezer and an apple and onion lying around. It tastes amazing and makes you feel very full after eating. I usually serve this with a very light salad.

Spectacular Taco Spice

By Alanna Rose Whitney

www.instructables.com/id/Spectacular-Taco-Spice/

Why buy taco seasoning at the store when you can make your own at home that is much more flavorful? It's extremely easy to do—read below to see how!

Step 1: Ingredients

Mix together the following:

- ½ tsp. cayenne pepper
- ⅛ tsp. (pinch) celery salt
- ½ tsp. chili powder
- ½ tsp. cumin
- 1 tsp. garlic powder
- 1 tsp. onion powder
- ½ tsp. paprika
- ⅛ tsp. (pinch) sea salt
- ½ tsp. turmeric

Step 2: Use It!

To use the taco spice, sprinkle a liberal amount over raw meat, such as ground beef, before cooking and mix in as it simmers.

Step 3: Store

Store in a spice jar or other small container.

Spicy Chickpeas with Feta and Oregano

By garnishrecipes

www.instructables.com/id/Spicy-Chickpeas-with-Feta-and-Oregano/

With a sprig of oregano from our patio herb garden, an extra nub of feta, and a sprinkle of intense cayenne, my limited supply of chickpeas became a simple yet satisfying dinner.

I added a squeeze of lemon to the beans and cayenne for a little extra tartness. You can toss the beans in a tablespoon of apple cider vinegar for the same effect if your cupboard happens to be lean that day.

This recipe serves 4.

Step 1: Ingredients

- 2 cups chickpeas, cooked
- 1 lemon, halved and seeded (or 1 tbsp. apple cider vinegar)
- 1 tbsp. olive oil
- ¼ tsp. cayenne pepper
- 3 tbsp. feta, crumbled
- 1 tbsp. oregano, finely chopped
- ¼ tsp. kosher salt
- Black pepper

Step 2: Instructions

Boil the chickpeas if necessary. A quick method for chickpeas (2 hours preparation time) is to bring them to a rolling boil for 2 minutes, let stand for 1 hour, then simmer for 1 hour. I like to add salt and a bay leaf to the chickpeas at the 45–minute mark.

When they're ready, toss them with one squeezed lemon, or the apple cider vinegar, and the tablespoon of olive oil. Add the cayenne and toss again.

Divide into a serving bowl, or four individual side dishes, and spoon the crumbled feta evenly over each bowl.

Finely chop the oregano leaves and distribute evenly as well.

Add a pinch of sea or kosher salt, a twist of pepper, and serve.

Desserts

- Gingered Hot Pepper Jelly
- My Ultimate Hot and Sweet Chili Garlic Ginger Jam
- Mexican Hot Chocolate Chip Cookies
- Mexican Hot Chocolate Cupcakes
- Sweet and Spicy Homemade Candied Ginger
- Spicy Orange Bourbon Sweet Potato Bread
- Apple Chips
- Peach and Turmeric Gelatin with Strawberry Coulis

Gingered Hot Pepper Jelly

By dracidephgm

www.instructables.com/id/Gingered-Hot-Pepper-Jelly/

In a previous instructable I showed how I make Minted Hot Pepper Jelly (see www.instructables.com/id/Minted-Hot-Pepper-Jelly). Late last summer we ran out of mint, but we still had hot peppers growing in a large quantity, so I decided to replace the mint with ginger. We really liked the outcome. This recipe is essentially the same as Minted Pepper Jelly with two exceptions:

Ginger is substituted for mint, and I try to use exclusively yellow, orange, or red hot peppers, while for the mint jelly I use green.

Step 1: Warning: Handling Hot Peppers

PLEASE, PLEASE, PLEASE use gloves when handling hot peppers. If the capsaicin (which is what makes the heat in chilis) gets in your eyes, you will be miserable for a while.

What increases the heat? Water washes away the oils or mucus that protects tissues and so will increase the heat from capsaicin. Anything that is salty or contains alcohol will increase the heat as well.

What decreases the heat? The fat in cold milk decreases the burning sensation. A cold sugar solution (10%) at 68°F is almost as effective.

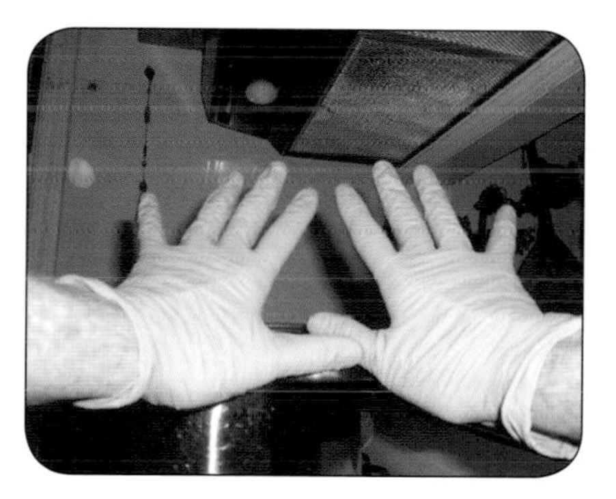

Step 2: Ingredients

- ¾ lb. mixed hot peppers, washed and chunked
- ⅓ cup fresh ginger, peeled
- 2 packets of low-sugar dry pectin
- 4 cups sugar (I often mix 2 cups sugar with the stevia equivalent of 2 cups sugar)
- 2 cups of 5% apple cider vinegar

Step 3: Mince the Pepper and Ginger

In a food processor finely mince the peppers with the ginger and set aside.

Step 4: Prepare the Pectin

Mix the dry pectin with about ½ cup of sugar and set aside.

Step 5: In a Medium Pot . . .

Mix the vinegar and remaining sugar. Add the minced peppers and ginger to the pot, then boil for 10 minutes over medium heat, stirring periodically to prevent burning.

Step 6: Add the Pectin Mixture

Remove the pot from heat. Add the pectin-sugar mixture to the pot and stir briskly. Return the mix to the heat and boil hard for 1 minute, stirring constantly.

Step 7: Check for Proper Gel

Chill a metal tablespoon by setting it in an ice water bath. Take a half spoonful of the pepper mix and let it cool on top of the ice to room temperature.

If it thickens up to the consistency of jelly it is ready. If not, mix in a little more pectin (about ⅓ to ½ of another package) and bring to a boil for 1 minute or cook a bit longer.

Step 8: Fill Sterile Jars

For the pepper jelly I use eight 12-ounce jars. I prepare the jars by running them and their caps through the dishwasher. They can also be boiled in a large pot prior to filling.

Fill jars to within ⅛ inch of the top and screw on covers tightly. Place in boiling bath for 10 minutes and cool. Once cooled, the caps should be concave.

Enjoy!

My Ultimate Hot and Sweet Chili Garlic Ginger Jam

By chipbuttiesandnoodlesoup

www.instructables.com/id/how-to-make-my-ultimate-hot-and-sweet-chilli-garli/

I am slightly addicted to chili and eat it on as many foods as possible. This is a spicy and sweet chili jam with garlic and ginger. I think it has a bit of a spicy kick, but it is not mouth burning, and you can still taste all the individual flavors. You can make it less hot by deseeding or using a milder chili. I hope you enjoy. This makes a great gift. I love this sauce on noodles or rice dishes, but it's also great in a cheese sandwich! It's also good to add into pasta sauces or stews while cooking to add a little chili hit to your recipes.

Step 1: Ingredients

- 225 g chili peppers (I used small green Thai/finger chilis, but any would work—you can deseed them if you want, but I did not as I wanted the extra heat)
- 400 g red bell pepper, cleaned, deseeded, and roughly chopped
- 600 g onion, chopped
- 1 head garlic, cloves peeled
- 50 g ginger
- 400 g tin chopped tomatoes
- 750 ml white or red wine vinegar (cider vinegar is also good)
- 1 tbsp. sea salt
- 1.5 kg sugar

Preparation time: 20 minutes.

Cooking time: 45–60 minutes (depending on pan size and heat).

Step 2: Prepare Your Veggies

Clean the chilis and peppers well and destalk the chilis. You may want to wear rubber gloves while doing this to protect your hands, and remember not to touch any sensitive body parts after handling chilis!

Add the cleaned and prepared chilis, peppers, onions, garlic, and ginger to a large pan with the tomatoes, vinegar, and salt and blend with a hand blender (or in an electric blender before putting in the pan, if you don't have one) until well mixed together. Keep your eyes out of the way, as any splashes would be very painful!

Step 3: Boil the Jam

Add the sugar, stir with a wooden spoon, and bring to a rolling boil for about 45–60 minutes until thickened and the wooden spoon leaves a trail when stirred in the bottom on the pan

Skim off any "scum" that rises to the surface.

Step 4: Prepare and Sterilize Your Jars

While the jam is boiling away sterilize your jars (when you have about 30 minutes to go). You will need enough jars for about 1,500—1,750 ml of finished product. (I used a combination of ½-liter kilner jars and small preserving jars with lids.)

You can use your preferred method of sterilization, but what I did was clean the jars and lids well in very hot, soapy water, rinse in clean, hot running water, then put on baking trays in an oven preheated to 350°F for 25–30 minutes.

Step 5: Pour the Jam into Jars

When the jars are sterilized and the jam is cooked, carefully add the jam to the prepared jars. Remember you must add hot jam to the hot jars, otherwise the end product will not be sterilized and also the jars may crack. Seal the jars immediately and leave to cool before storing in a cool, dark place.

The jam is ready to eat the next day, but will also keep for at least one month unopened. Once opened, store in the fridge.

Mexican Hot Chocolate Chip Cookies

By Megan Bagley

www.instructables.com/id/Mexican-Hot-Chocolate-Chip-Cookies/

Or, as my boyfriend calls them, pepper doodles. Whatever you call them, they are really delicious cookies with a bit of a kick. I came up with the idea of these cookies after getting a chili-infused chocolate bar at the store on a whim and fell in love. To me it screamed to be baked into a cookie, but I felt a traditional chocolate chip cookie wasn't exactly the right fit; instead, I wanted a cookie that would complement the sweet and spicy chocolate without being too bland or overpowering. Cinnamon seemed to be the solution, playing off the distinct flavor combination of Mexican hot chocolate. So I set out to see if I could even make them, not knowing if they would be any good at all, and I am quite happy with the results. For those of you who aren't into spicy foods, these shouldn't be a challenge at all; the spice kicks in as a nice little afterburn that really just makes your mouth tingle a bit.

Step 1: Ingredients and Equipment

Ingredients:

- 2 bars of chili-infused chocolate (I used Lindt, but if you want to make this from scratch it is roughly 7 ounces)
- 1½ cups sugar
- ½ cup butter, softened
- 1 tsp. of vanilla extract
- 2 eggs
- 2¾ cups flour
- 1 tsp. baking soda
- ½ tsp. cream of tartar
- ¼ tsp. salt
- 1 tsp. cinnamon
- Pinch of cayenne pepper
- 2 tsp. cinnamon
- 2 tbsp. sugar
- Pinch of cayenne pepper

Equipment:

- Electric mixer, either a stand or hand mixer would work fine
- Chopping board
- Large knife
- Small extra bowl
- Parchment paper or cooking spray

Step 2: "Chipping" the Chocolate

There are plenty of great ways to go about doing this, probably some easier than the way I ended up doing it, but this way seemed to work pretty well for me.

Lay the chocolate bar on the cutting board. Use a long knife to press into chocolate, holding onto the handle and applying pressure on the blade. Using the knife like a see-saw, rock the pressure back and forth to cut the chocolate into strips. Turn the cutting board and, using the same method, cut in the opposite direction until the chocolate is roughly chip sized. I like to vary the size of the chunks from very small to the size of a dime. I also like a lot of chocolate chips in each cookie, but feel free to vary the amount to your preference.

If you have a stand mixer or a second set of helping hands, you can do this while the dough is mixing.

Step 3: Mixing the Dough

Preheat the oven to 400°F.

Combine the 1½ cups sugar, butter, vanilla extract, and eggs. Mix well.

In a separate bowl, sift together the flour, baking soda, cream of tartar, salt, 1 tsp. cinnamon, and cayenne pepper. Mix into the sugar mixture.

Add the chocolate and mix until integrated.

Step 4: Forming the Cookies

In a small bowl, mix together the remaining ingredients, 2 tbsp. sugar, 2 tsp. cinnamon, and pinch of cayenne pepper. This will be the powdered coating for the cookies.

The dough isn't that sticky and can easily be handled. Form the dough into balls roughly the size of a ping-pong ball. Roll each ball in the cinnamon-sugar mixture.

Arrange balls roughly 1½ to 2 inches apart on a prepared cookie sheet (lined with parchment paper or sprayed with cooking spray). 1 ½ to 2 inches apart on a prepared cookie sheet (sprayed with cookie spray or lined with parchment paper).

This recipe should make 20–22 cookies. Bake cookies for 8–10 min. When they are done, immediately move them to a cooling rack. Let them cool for a bit, then eat and enjoy. Cookies are best warm out of the oven with a tall glass of milk.

Mexican Hot Chocolate Cupcakes

By wold630

www.instructables.com/id/Mexican-Hot-Chocolate-Cupcakes/

My entire family loves hot peppers. We grow habaneros, jalapeños, scotch bonnets, and cayenne peppers in our garden and use them on a regular basis. Even my three-year-old has recently graduated to habanero salsa. He eats it in small amounts, of course, but he loves the floral flavor like the rest of us.

I lived in the Southwest for many years of my life and regretfully never tried an authentic Mexican hot chocolate. I thought it would be a great idea to try it for the first time in cupcake form. Since my whole family loves spice, these are extra spicy with a candied cayenne pepper garnish!

The flavor is spectacular! Seriously delicious! The spice is balanced out by the sweetness of the chocolate, and the added cinnamon brings it to a whole new level. I never thought chocolate and cinnamon would be great together, but I was horribly wrong. It is so, so good!

There are a lot of small steps for this cupcake, but all are worth the effort.

Step 1: Candied Cayenne Peppers

Candied peppers are so easy to make and are a deliciously spicy topper for these cupcakes.

You will need:

- 5–7 cayenne peppers
- ½ cup water
- ½ cup sugar, plus more for rolling

Cut cayenne peppers in half and remove membranes and seeds. Cut off stem and cut into slices of desired size.

Bring water, sugar, and peppers to a boil in a small saucepan. Reduce heat and simmer about 20 minutes or until liquid reduces to a thick syrup. Remove peppers and roll in sugar to coat. Place on a silpat mat to cool and harden.

Note: Use caution when cutting hot peppers. I recommend wearing gloves unless you know exactly how to handle the peppers. The oils will get on your skin and burn if you are not careful.

Step 2: Make Cupcakes

You will need:

- 1½ cups flour
- ½ cup sugar
- ¼ cup brown sugar
- ½ cup cocoa powder
- 1-oz. pkg. (favorite) hot chocolate
- ¼ tsp. salt
- 1½ tsp. baking soda
- 1½ tsp. cayenne powder
- 1 tsp. cinnamon powder

- ¾ cup milk
- 3 tbsp. olive oil
- 1½ tsp. vanilla
- 2 eggs
- ½ cup hot water

Preheat oven to 350°F. Line 18 muffin cups with liners.

In a large mixing bowl, combine the flour, sugars, cocoa powder, hot chocolate mix, salt, baking soda, and spices.

In the bowl of a stand mixer fitted with a paddle attachment add the milk, olive oil, vanilla, and eggs. Mix well.

Add in the dry ingredients a little at a time until well mixed. Stream in hot water while the mixer is running.

Batter will be thin, but this will result in an extremely moist cupcake! Pour batter into liners until halfway full and bake approximately 25 minutes or until toothpick inserted comes out clean.

Let cupcakes cool completely on a wire rack.

Step 3: Make Whipped Cream

You will need:

- 1 cup heavy cream
- 3 tbsp. sugar
- 1 tsp. vanilla

In the bowl of a stand mixer fitted with a whisk attachment add cream, sugar, and vanilla and whisk on medium-high until stiff peaks form. Do not over beat.

Spoon whipped cream into a piping bag fitted with a large star tip. Squeeze a generous amount onto the cooled cupcakes to form a little mountain, like you would get on top of your hot chocolate.

Step 4: Marshmallows and Chocolate

I don't know if authentic Mexican hot chocolate is traditionally served with marshmallows and chocolate, but my cupcakes couldn't be served without them!

Cut the sides off of marshmallows to get petal-like shapes. You will get three out of each marshmallow. Set aside.

Using a vegetable peeler, scrape along the side of a chocolate bar to get little curls of chocolate. About ¼ to ½ of a chocolate bar will be plenty.

Step 5: Assemble

Gently dust the cream-topped cupcakes with cinnamon powder. Add two pieces of candied cayenne, one marshmallow piece and several chocolate shavings.

Eat and enjoy!

Sweet and Spicy Homemade Candied Ginger

By Lindsay Ponta

www.instructables.com/id/Sweet-Spicy-Homemade-Candied-Ginger/

Crystallized (or candied) ginger is a great addition to baked goods, trail mix, or even as a chewy snack with a bit of a kick. You can buy it already candied at many grocery stores, but it's way, way cheaper to make it yourself. I like to think it's a lot more satisfying, too!

Step 1: What You Need

- 1/2 lb. fresh ginger root
- Granulated sugar
- Water
- Vegetable peeler
- Sharp knife

Step 2: Peel Away

Cut the ginger into pieces and peel all the skin off each piece.

Step 3: Slice and Dice

Slice each piece thinly—no more than ⅛-inch thick.

Step 4: Turn Up the Heat

Boil all the pieces over medium-high heat for about 45 minutes until they're softer and no longer crisp.

Drain the water from the pot, keeping 1/8 cup water in the pot with the ginger.

To the ginger and water, add sugar in approximately the same amount as your ginger. Stir together and boil it down until it evaporates and starts to look like sugar grains again. Stir constantly to keep everything separated and evenly coated.

Step 5: Dry It Out

Put all the pieces on a cooling rack to dry.

Spicy Orange Bourbon Sweet Potato Bread

By annahowardshaw

www.instructables.com/id/Spicy-Orange-Bourbon-Sweet-Potato-Bread/

Bring this to your next barbecue or picnic for a surprisingly spicy dessert! When I make sweet potatoes as a side dish, I add orange juice, garlic, and cayenne. But when I made sweet potato bread, it was essentially a banana bread recipe substituting sweet potato for the bananas.

I played around with the recipe to tailor it to sweet potatoes specifically. And, more specifically, to incorporate the elements from the crazy-hot version of sweet potatoes I tend to make. It blends the sweet/salty/spicy elements of the side dish but in quick bread form. The bread itself has a light chili flavor with a strong cayenne kick from the candied pecan topping. If you are a fan of the sweet/spicy combo, you will most certainly dig this. Enjoy!

Step 1: Ingredients

Candied Pecans:

- ½ cup granulated sugar
- ¼ cup maple syrup
- 1 tbsp. brown sugar
- 1 tbsp. bourbon
- 1 tsp. orange zest
- ½ tsp. salt
- ½ tsp. cinnamon
- ½ tsp. cayenne
- 2 cups pecans

Bread:

- 1½ cups flour
- 1 cup cooked sweet potato, mashed
- 1 cup granulated sugar
- ½ cup brown sugar
- ½ cup canola cup oil
- ½ cup fresh orange juice
- ¼ cup bourbon
- ¼ cup flax seed, ground
- 2 eggs
- 1 tbsp. minced chilies (rehydrated Mexican red chili)
- 1 tsp. baking powder
- 1 tsp. baking soda
- 1 tsp. cinnamon
- 1 tsp. cayenne pepper
- ½ tsp. nutmeg
- ¼ tsp. salt

Step 2: Begin with the Pecans

Combine all candied pecans ingredients (except pecans) into a saucepan. Heat slowly. Bring to a simmer, mix in pecans, then reduce heat. Mix for a minute. Pour onto parchment paper and set aside.

Step 3: Now for the Batter

Blend together all bread ingredients in a mixing bowl (I don't bother with separately mixing wet/dry ingredients for quick breads). Pour batter into lightly greased bread pan.

Step 4: Add Topping

Now that the pecans have dried a little, break them up and put the pieces on top of the batter. You will have more than enough pecans to cover the top, so press them down into the batter until they are all used. This will ensure that not all the topping will fall off when the bread is sliced.

Step 5: And Finally

Bake the bread at 350°F for 70–80 minutes.

Apple Chips

By panj

www.instructables.com/id/How-to-make-Apple-Chips/

These apple chips are a great snack for the fall season.

Step 1: What You'll Need

- Sugar
- Ground cinnamon
- Ground cloves
- Apple
- Parchment paper
- Baking sheets
- Large mixing bowl

Step 2: Mix Your Ingredients

Preheat the oven to 300°F.

In a small bowl, mix the sugar, cinnamon, and clove together. The ratio I used is 4 tsp. sugar to 1 tsp. each cinnamon and clove.

Step 3: Slice Up the Apples

Quarter the apple and cut it into equally thick slices. It is very important that they are all the same (relative) thickness.

Note: if you plan on making a large batch, do not slice all the apples at once, as they will start to turn brown very quickly.

Put the slices in a large mixing bowl.

Step 4: Spice Up the Apples!

Sprinkle the spice mixture heavily over the apple slices and stir the batch with a spoon until they are coated evenly.

Step 5: Get Ready for the Oven

Place the spiced apple slices on a baking sheet lined with parchment paper. Make sure none are overlapping.

Step 6: Put 'em in the Oven

Bake for about 45 minutes.

I experimented with higher temperature and less time, but always ended up with a half burned or half un-crisp batch.

Check on them after half an hour. And while you're waiting . . . make another batch!

Step 7: Eat

Remove from the oven. They will continue to crisp after you take them out. Peel them off the parchment paper. They should be crispy just like any other chip.

Enjoy!

Peach and Turmeric Gelatin with Strawberry Coulis

By cerqueic

www.instructables.com/id/Peach-and-Turmeric-Gelatin-with-Strawberry-Coulis/

Fresh turmeric gives these peaches a ginger-like taste. Turmeric is usually paired with cardamom and coriander in curries. But when mixed with the subtleties of peach, sugar, and white wine, it stops being curry's underwhelming filler and becomes a robust flavor driver.

If you don't eat it for its decadence, eat it for turmeric—the spice dessert forgot.

Step 1: Ingredients and Tools

Ingredients for peach gelatin:

- 2–3 ripe peaches
- ½ tsp. fresh turmeric, finely chopped (powdered has a very different taste)
- ⅓ cup white wine
- 1 packet of gelatin
- ¼ cup white sugar
- ½ cup water

Ingredients for the rustic coulis:

- 10 strawberries
- 2 tbsp. sugar
- ¼ cup white wine
- 1 lemon, for juice and decorations

Tools:

- Food processor
- Mixing bowl
- Saucepan
- Peeler
- Knife
- Jell-o molds/baking pan/ serving glasses

Step 2: Prepare the Gelatin

Peel and chop the peaches. Puree in a food processor.

Slice off a small chunk of turmeric. Cut off the skin and finely chop to ½ tsp.

Pour ¼ cup of the peach puree into a saucepan on low heat and add the turmeric, wine, gelatin, and sugar. Whisk the ingredients together quickly, making sure the gelatin is well integrated. You may need to add a tablespoon or two of water.

Heat for five minutes until it has warmed through. Don't let boil or overheat.

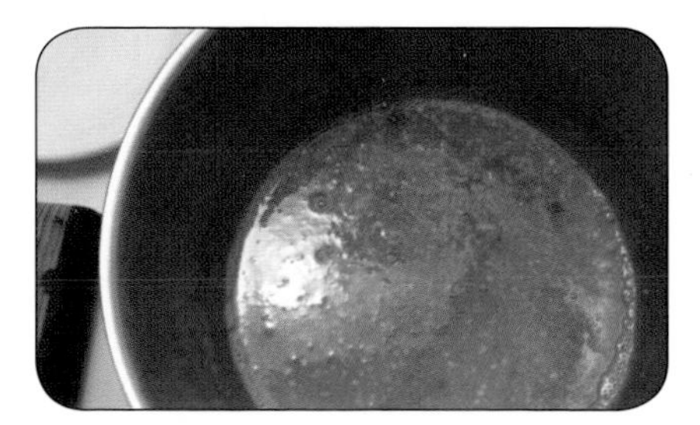

Step 3: Preparing the Gelatin, Part 2

Pour the peach and turmeric mixture into a mixing bowl. Add remaining puree and water. Mix together and quickly pour into your molds, glasses, or baking pan. If you use a pan, you can cut the gelatin into squares. Molds are sometimes hard to break loose, but look nice if done well. Cover with plastic wrap and cool in the fridge for several hours.

Step 4: Making a Rustic Coulis

Prepare the coulis about a half hour before you serve the gelatin. This recipe is flexible. You should adjust it to the amount you want to use for flavor and decoration.

Puree about 10 strawberries. Place in a saucepan and add the sugar, wine, and juice from a good squeeze of a lemon half. Heat on low to medium heat. The mixture should simmer lightly, but not reach a rousing boil. After the mixture thickens and reduces by about half (about 10–15 minutes), remove from heat and let cool a bit.

Remove the peach gelatin from the fridge. Pour on the coulis. You can decorate by creating lemon julienne strips. (Slice a lemon in half and use a peeler to peel the edge ring. Twist into a curl.)

Step 5: Serving

Arrange with flair. Serve with strawberries. Invite discerning guests.

Drinks

Homemade Ginger Ale

By mediaphage

www.instructables.com/id/Homemade-ginger-ale/

I've made my own ginger ale for years, and here's how.

Step 1: Ingredients and Tools

You'll need:

- Small piece of ginger root
- 1 cup sugar (or less)
- Yeast
- 1 lemon
- A grater (microplane or fine holes) or food processor/ chopper
- An empty 2-liter plastic (important) bottle
- 2 liters fresh water

Step 2: Ginger Root Preparation

Peel and finely grate a small piece of ginger. How much is up to you; it depends on how strong you want the final ginger ale to be. Try for 1 tablespoon or so in the beginning, and if you want it stronger, add another half tablespoon; weaker, add less. I didn't measure the amount I used here, but I like it spicy, and it came out fairly strong.

Step 3: Squeeze Lemon

I generally add a full lemon's worth of juice to this. If, like me, you don't have a juicer, roll the lemon between your hand and a hard surface a few times; this will help to get the juice out more quickly once it's cut.

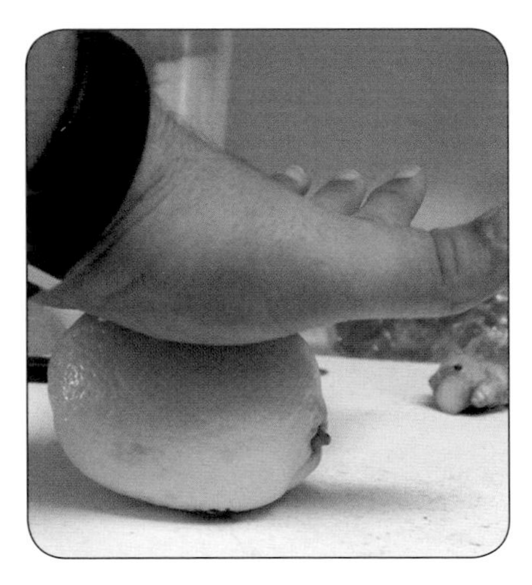

Step 4: Put Ingredients in Bottle

To the empty 2-liter bottle add:

- 1 cup sugar (Again, taste comes into play. I like it less sweet, so I add ¾ cup. You may wish to add more or less depending on your personal taste. Add a full cup the first time you make it, and go from there).
- ¼ tsp. yeast
- Lemon juice
- Grated ginger

If you're having difficulty with the sugar and juice, make a funnel out of a paper plate to pour everything in. Once everything's together, shake it around a little to distribute things. If you're really paranoid about germs, you could prepare a weak bleach solution and rinse everything with it, but I don't see the point since you'll likely drink this before anything goes wrong. Just be sure to wash your hands before you touch stuff and you'll be fine.

Step 5: Biological Carbonation

Fill your 2-liter bottle to an inch or two below the top with fresh water. Screw the cap on tightly and shake until everything is dispersed. Be certain to flush the sugar from the nooks at the bottom of the bottle. The picture below shows everything in the bottle before it's been shaken. Once you're finished, place the bottle in a warm-ish place (I set mine on top of the fridge, towards the back) and let it steep. Check on it every few hours by squeezing the bottle. When you can no longer push in on the bottle (i.e., it's become pressurized), put it in the fridge. This will slow down the fermentation and keep things from exploding. It never takes more than a day or so for me, but depending on how you vary the ingredients, things may take a little longer.

Note: I am quite serious about the exploding bit. If you leave the bottle just sitting in a warm place for a few days, it will likely explode and send sugary water all over the room. Keep an eye on it!

Step 6: Enjoy!

This stuff is best really cold. As with any yeast-based product, this will yield a tiny amount of alcohol in the final product. Really, I think it's less than one percent. You could easily drink the entire bottle and not have any issues. Those with allergies to alcohol, however, may want to be careful.

Lion's Milk

By Doga Ozesmi

www.instructables.com/id/Lions-Milk/

Lion's milk is a tasty concoction of spices, milk, and honey. I like to have a cup before I go to bed or in the afternoon with a cookie or other sweet.

Step 1: Ingredients

- ¼ tsp. cinnamon
- ¼ tsp. turmeric
- ¼ tsp. cardamom
- 2 cups whole milk
- Honey to taste

Step 2: Instructions

Whisk the spices together in the milk and bring to a boil. Stand next to the pot because it foams up and will spill over unless the heat is turned off. Pour yourself a cup and add honey to taste.

Enjoy!

Making a Probiotic Ginger Beer

By rdoherty

www.instructables.com/id/Making-a-Probiotic-Ginger-Beer/

Incorporate probiotic bacteria into ginger-based beverages! Yum. With some simple ingredients, a few items from around the kitchen, and about 2–3 weeks you can have your own DIY probiotic ginger beer.

Step 1: Ingredients

- Filtered water
- Ginger root
- Evaporated cane sugar
- Sugar
- Juice of 2 lemons

Step 2: Starting the Ginger Bug

Place 1 cup of filtered water in a pint jar. Add 2 teaspoons of freshly grated ginger root (skin and all). Stir in 2 teaspoons of evaporated cane sugar, tighten lid, and shake.

Cover (I use a coffee filter and rubber band) and store in a warm place. Add 2 teaspoons of cane sugar and ginger root each day. In 2–7 days, when it starts bubbling, it is active and ready for the next step.

Use right away for best results.

Step 3: Making the Ginger Beer

Bring 2 quarts of water to a boil. Add about 2 inches of ginger root, grated, for a mild flavor (up to 6 inches of ginger for a more intense flavor). Add 1 ½ cups of sugar. Boil the mixture for about 15 minutes. Let mixture come to room temperature, and when it is cool strain the ginger out.

Add the juice of two lemons, then add the strained ginger bug. Now add enough water to make it 1 gallon. Ginger beer does not tolerate chlorinated water. Tap water left out overnight or mineral water should be fine.

Transfer from mason jar to sealable bottle using a funnel. Leave to ferment in a warm place for about two weeks. Refrigerate before opening.

Step 4: Bottle Your Ginger Beer

When bottling, use sealable bottles. Screw-top recycled plastic bottles, rubber gasket-style or gallon jug jars can be used.

Rhizome Sodas

By taylorwolf

www.instructables.com/id/Rhizome-Sodas/

Inspired by Sandor Katz's *The Art of Fermentation*, I wanted to make some soda flavors I've never had before. According to Katz, a soda can be made by adding an active starter culture (in this case, whey derived from yogurt) to any sweetened liquid. I thought I'd riff on ginger ale and make sodas from fresh turmeric and galangal, ginger's rhizomatic relatives.

Step 1: Gather Whey

Whey can be derived from any cultured milk product, including kefir, buttermilk, raw milk, and yogurt. Kefir, buttermilk, and raw milk will naturally separate into curds and whey after sitting unrefrigerated for a few days. But if you collect whey by straining yogurt, not only is the whey available immediately, but the yogurt becomes labneh: a tangier, thick, and spreadable yogurt. Line a bowl with a few layers of cheesecloth and empty some yogurt into it. A 32 oz. tub of Nancy's yogurt yields around 2 cups of whey. Close up the package of yogurt and suspend it so the whey can freely drip out. If your bowl is deep enough, you can lay a wooden spoon across it and tie the cheesecloth sack to the spoon. It won't take long to get enough whey for the sodas, but I set mine up overnight for the sake of the labneh.

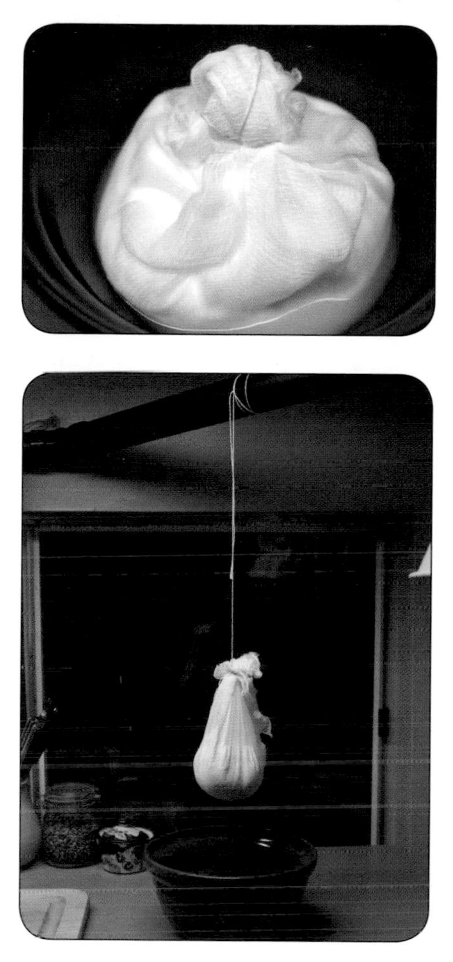

Step 2: Brew Decoction

Using a microplane, grate turmeric into one pot and galangal into the other. For each soda, I steeped 100 g of rhizome in 6 cups of water, but you have a lot of leeway with these numbers. Bring each pot to a boil, then cover and simmer for about 15 minutes. Taste it at this point—if the decoction comes out too strong, you can water it down; if it's a bit weak, make a smaller, concentrated batch to add to the original batch.

Step 3: Strain Decoction

When you're happy with the decoction's concentration, strain it into a jar or bowl. I used a mesh fabric bag I bought at a brew store, but a few layers of cheesecloth or a metal strainer would do the job as well. While the liquid is still hot, add sugar, tasting as you go until it's the right sweetness for you. I ended up adding about 1 cup of sugar to 6 cups of liquid. Heat kills the living cultures in the yogurt, so let the decoctions cool off to room temperature, either on the counter or in the fridge.

Step 4: Add Whey to Decoctions

Once your decoctions are cool, add the whey at a ratio of roughly ¼ cup whey for every 4 cups liquid. The decoctions have been brought to life! Stir them up and cover with some cheesecloth. Allow the cultures to get nice and active by letting them sit out for a day at room temperature.

Step 5: Transfer to Sealable Bottles

Once they appear active, transfer to sealable containers and close them off. Crack open a lid after a couple days to gauge how much carbonation has built up. Once they're bubbly enough for you, refrigerate and drink up!

The Most Awesome Gløgg Ever

By Solskinner

www.instructables.com/id/The-Most-Awesome-Glogg-Ever/

I lived in Denmark for a few years, and one of the best drinks I had while living there was gløgg. Gløgg is a warm holiday drink that not only warms the body, but is very tasty too. If you are having a gathering this holiday season, prepare this and your guests will love it. In fact, even if you aren't having a gathering, prepare it; you'll be glad you did. Enjoy!

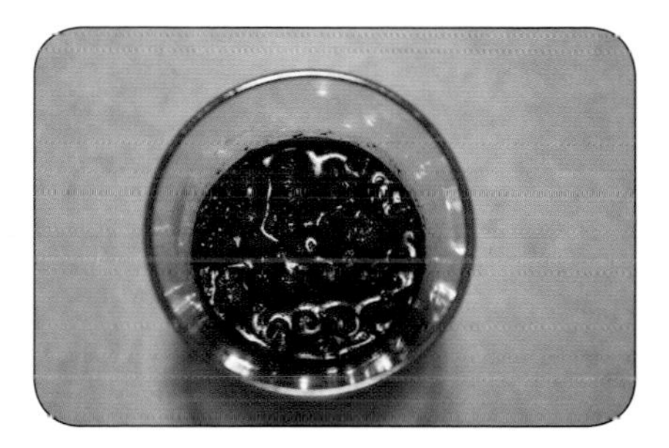

Step 1: What You Need

- Crock-pot or any other pot you can use to simmer the gløgg
- Cheesecloth
- 1 bottle red wine
- 1 cup port wine
- 1 orange—you will use the peel for zest
- 1 tbsp. whole cloves
- Cinnamon sticks
- 1 cup raw almonds (blanched or whole)

The wine and port do not have to be of the highest quality because they will be mixed in with everything else.

Step 2: Add the Wine

First, open the red wine and pour the entire bottle into the crock pot, which has not been turned on.

If you are using a pot, pour the entire bottle into the pot. Make sure there is enough room in the pot to accommodate two bottles of wine. You won't be including two bottles, but you will ensure that you have enough room in your pot.

Putting the wine in before everything else allows it to breathe while you are preparing the other things to go into the gløgg.

I am by no means a wine snob, so I think even a twist-off variety of red wine would be okay for this recipe. I have never tried it, but if you do let me know what it tastes like.

Step 3: Add the Port Wine

Open the port wine and pour one cup into the pot. You can add more port wine later. At this point, do not introduce heat.

Step 4: Make the Orange Zest!

Using a vegetable peeler, knife, or anything else you have, cut a thin layer off the orange peel. Make sure not to get the pith, which will make the gløgg bitter. You will want to peel the entire orange. This is the orange zest!

Step 5: Prepare the Spice Sachet Using the Cheesecloth

Now you will want to cut about 6 inches of the cheesecloth. It does not need to be exact, but you will be putting the cloves and the orange zest in it. Cheesecloth comes folded in several layers, as you can see in the photo on the next page, so you will just cut across all the layers. The piece will be 6 inches wide but very long.

Step 6: Put the Cloves and Orange Zest Together

Measure one tablespoon of the cloves and place in a pile with the orange zest on the center of the cheesecloth you cut. This will be the mixture you use for the spice sachet.

Step 7: Make the Spice Sachet

Now that the cloves and oranges are on the center of the cheesecloth, just tie up the sachet. I double-wrapped mine. The reason you want to make the sachet is so that the cloves and zest are not floating around in the actual drink, but rather are used for flavoring.

Step 8: Turn on the Crock-Pot or Stove

At this point, you should turn on your heat source to a simmer. If using a crock pot, put on low; if using a stove, heat the wine and port mixture to a simmer.

Step 9: Add the Cinnamon Sticks

Add two cinnamon sticks directly into the wine mixture. I used two cinnamon sticks, but they were about twice as long and thick as regular ones, so you can adjust accordingly.

Step 10: Add the Sachet to the Wine Mixture

Carefully place the sachet into the wine mixture.

Step 11: Chop Up the Almonds

Take 1 cup of almonds and chop them up. Of course you can also buy blanched or pre-chopped almonds, but I like big pieces so I chop them myself. You can chop them to any size, but do not make them too small or they will be like sediment at the bottom of the mixture.

Step 12: Measure Out the Golden Raisins and Add to Chopped Almonds

Take 1 cup of golden raisins and add them to the almonds.

Step 13: Add the Raisins and Almonds to the Wine Mixture

Step 14: Add the Sugar to the Wine Mixture and Turn Up the Heat!

Step 15: Now Is the Time to Add More Sugar or Port Wine

Now that the gløgg has had a chance to simmer, you can taste to see if you would like to add more sugar or more port wine.

Step 16: Ladle and Serve

The gløgg can now be served. Make sure you add almonds and raisins to the bottom of the glass; they will have soaked up the flavor of the gløgg quite nicely. And, yes, do eat the almonds and raisins; that's the best part to me!

Natural Remedies

- Cinnamon-Swirl Coffee Scrub
- Warm Cinnamon Mask
- Garlic Remedies
- Homemade Shampoo
- Home Remedy for Burns
- Make Your Skin Glow with Sandalwood Paste
- Remedy for Losing Your Voice: Cayenne Cure

Cinnamon-Swirl Coffee Scrub

By Jessica Reddick Gatlin

www.instructables.com/id/Cinnamon-Swirl-Coffee-Scrub/

If you're ever looking for a quick gift, then I've got the perfect one for you to turn to. Cinnamon-Swirl Coffee Scrub! Everyone loves homemade gifts. This scrub is wonderful for hostesses, secretaries, bosses, assistants at your doctor's office, teachers, neighbors, and as shower favors. The recipe even doubles like a charm! Perfect, right?

Step 1: Ingredients

- 2 cups coffee grounds, unbrewed
- ½ cup turbinado sugar
- 6 tbsp. olive oil
- 1 tsp. ground cinnamon
- 2–3 drops cinnamon fragrance oil
- 2 (½-liter) glass containers with lids

Step 2: Instructions

In a large bowl, mix all ingredients together. Using a spatula, transfer mix into the container and secure lid. Tie a ribbon and a tag onto the jar with these instructions:

"Scoop a teaspoon or two of the scrub on your hands and gently massage in circular motions onto your skin. Leave on for 3 to 4 minutes before thoroughly rinsing. The scrub will tighten a bit on your skin."

Recipe originally published on My Baking Heart: http://mybakingheart.com

Warm Cinnamon Mask

By SweetGirlHelp

www.instructables.com/id/DIY-Warm-Cinnamon-Mask/

This mask is absolutely great!

It smells fantastic, only uses three simple household ingredients, and it works immediately. How does this mask work? Well, the honey works as an antibacterial and reduces redness, the cinnamon shrinks the size of pores, and the nutmeg minimizes swelling and inflammation. To be completely honest, I was a little skeptical while putting on this mask. But when I rinsed it off and saw how much better my skin looked, I knew this recipe had to be shared! Follow these steps to have almost flawlessly smooth skin.

Note: Please don't use this mask if you are allergic to honey, cinnamon, or nutmeg!

Step 1: Ingredients

- 2 tbsp. of honey
- 1½ tsp. of cinnamon
- 1 tsp. of nutmeg

Other items you will need:

- 1 small towel
- Headband (if your hair is long)
- Face wash or soap (depending on your skin type)
- 1 bowl
- Spoon

Step 2: Honey

Time to get cooking! Measure out 2 tablespoons of honey and put it into your bowl.

Quick Fix: If the honey is a little too thick and won't come out of the bottle, pop the entire bottle into the microwave for 20 seconds. But be sure to watch it in the microwave, as honey melts fast!

Step 3: Cinnamon

Add the cinnamon to your mixture. Make sure to add no more than 1½ teaspoons because cinnamon is a very strong spice and any more than this can be too harsh for your skin.

Step 4: Nutmeg

Carefully stir in the nutmeg. Again, don't add too much, because the scent can be a little overwhelming when sitting on your face.

Step 5: Check Your Mixture

Now your mixture should look like the top right picture. If it's too thick, add more honey. If it's too thin, add more cinnamon. But do not add more nutmeg!

Step 6: Wash Your Face

Remove all makeup and creams from your skin before applying the mask. You never know how some chemicals may react to this mask so, just to be safe, wash your face really well.

Step 7: Apply the Mask

Apply a thick layer of this all over your face, except around your eyes and mouth. Be sure to get the mask along the sides of your jaw. If you have long hair or bangs, be sure to pin it back. This mask is super sticky and is extremely hard to wash out of hair!

Step 8: Relax for 30 Minutes

Now let the mask sit for 30 minutes. While waiting you can clean up your mess, finish up homework, or just listen to music.

Step 9: Rinse

Rinse off the mask using a circular motion, which will exfoliate the skin.

Step 10: Pat Dry

Dry your face with a towel. Look at your skin! Happy with the results? Another great thing about this mask is that it leaves a little bit of a cinnamon scent on your skin for a while!

Step 11: Store Mask

Now, you can store your mask in the fridge. Just make sure you put a cover on the container or bowl you store it in. You can keep this mask for up to 5 days. If this mask dried your skin out, dab a little bit of moisturizing cream on the dry spots. You are finished!

Garlic Remedies

By lamefreaks

www.instructables.com/id/Garlic-Remidies/

Home remedies are the age-old practices that have been passed on through generations. Basic stuff like fruits, vegetables, grains, and so on possess medicinal virtues. As we are using natural ingredients, it does not cause any kind of side effect, which is kind of common in modern drugs.

The natural ingredient I'm showcasing here is garlic. I hate garlic, as it gives a foul smell to your breath, but garlic is a great remedy for common ailments. I have listed various uses of garlic in this Instructable. I hope it is of great use to you!

Step 1: Remedy for Backache

Ingredients:

- Garlic
- Any kind of oil that is used as a rubefacient (mustard oil, coconut oil, sesame oil)

The oil is prepared by frying 10 cloves of garlic in 60 ml of oil in a frying pan. Here I've used coconut oil. They have to be fried on a low flame till they are brown. After the oil has cooled, it should be applied vigorously on the back and has to remain there for about three hours. After that the person may take a warm bath. This should be continued for at least 10–15 days for best results.

Step 2: Remedy for Common Cold

About 4–5 cloves of garlic should be chopped and boiled in a cup of water. You can add salt for taste. The medicinal properties of the garlic in the soup flushes down all the toxins in the body, thus reducing the severity of your cold. This should be taken once every day.

Step 3: Remedy for Earache

Three cloves of garlic should be warmed up and then mashed with a pinch of salt. This mix should be wrapped in a woolen cloth and placed on the painful ear.

In a second remedy, use garlic oil. If it is not available, take 3 cloves of peeled garlic and heat it in a tbsp. of any sweet oil except groundnut oil. Heat it until the garlic has charred and the oil has turned brown. Then this oil has to be cooled and filtered. Put a few drops of the oil into the affected ear. This will give instant relief.

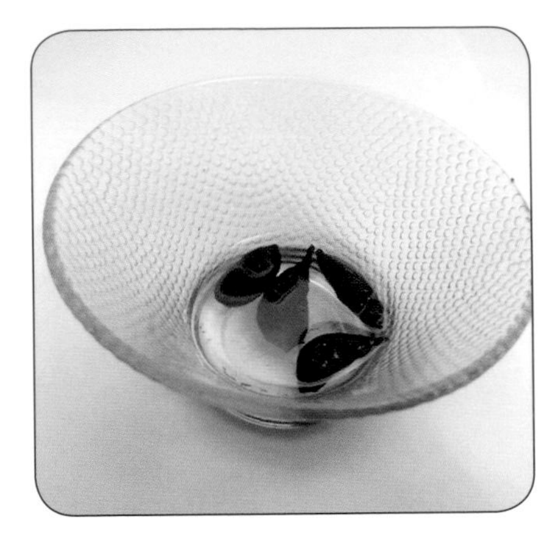

Step 4: Remedy for Toothache

A clove of garlic with a little rock salt should be placed on the affected tooth. It will relieve the pain. For best results you should chew a garlic clove every morning, which will keep your teeth healthy and strong.

Homemade Shampoo

By scoochmaroo

www.instructables.com/id/Homemade-Shampoo/

This is your ultimate guide to homemade shampoo! Here are ten easy recipes you can use to find the perfect formula for your hair.

The benefits are that you can use all-natural ingredients, avoid all of the fillers and irritants commercial makers use, scent it any way you want, and customize it to suit your hair's needs. What more do I need to say?

This mixture isn't as thick as commercial shampoos; you'll need to just tilt the bottle over your head. I am really impressed with how much lather I get from it though!

Recipe 1: Basic

For normal hair, or as a base to add your own scents, use:

- ¼ cup distilled water
- ¼ cup liquid castile soap—I use unscented, but you can choose your favorite
- ½ tsp. jojoba, grapeseed, or other light vegetable oil
- Flip-cap bottles or foaming bottles to dispense

Mix together all the ingredients. Store in a bottle. Shake before use.

Recipe 2: Stimulate

To wake up your scalp and your senses, try tea tree and peppermint oil! This one's my personal favorite, and the one I use daily. It's so refreshing!

Combine:

- ¼ cup distilled water
- ¼ cup liquid castile soap—I use unscented, but you can choose your favorite
- 2 tsp. jojoba oil

- ⅛ tsp. peppermint essential oil
- ⅛ tsp. tea tree essential oil
- Flip-cap bottles or foaming bottles to dispense

Mix all ingredients, then add ¼ cup distilled water. Store in a bottle. Use as you would any shampoo, and rinse well.

Recipe 3: Quench

For dry hair, try this:

- ¼ cup distilled water
- ¼ cup liquid castile soap, your favorite scent
- ¼ cup aloe vera gel
- 1 tsp. glycerin
- ¼ tsp. avocado oil or jojoba oil
- Flip-cap bottles or foaming bottles to dispense

Mix together all the ingredients. Store in a bottle and always shake well before using. Apply to hair and allow to sit for a few minutes. Rinse well with cool water.

Recipe 4: Soothe

Chamomile makes this shampoo a calming treat. Chamomile also has natural lightening properties, so combine this with lemon juice if you want to lighten your hair!

You will need:

- 6 chamomile tea bags
- 1 cup distilled water
- 1 cup castile soap—try lavender!
- 1½ tbsp. glycerin
- Flip-cap bottles or foaming bottles to dispense

Steep the tea bags in 1 cup of boiled water for 20 minutes. Remove the tea bags and discard. Add castile soap to the tea. Stir in glycerin until well blended. Keep in a dark, cool place in a sealed bottle.

Recipe 5: De-flake

Dandruff can affect many different people in every age group. Dandruff can manifest as either very dry and flaky scalp or very oily scalp with flakes. Contrary to popular belief, dandruff is not caused by a dry scalp or from improper hair care. It can be caused by increased oil production, hormonal fluctuations, stress, and illness.

To banish a flaky scalp, try this simple recipe:

- ¼ cup distilled water
- ¼ cup liquid castile soap
- ½ tsp. jojoba, grapeseed, or other light vegetable oil
- 1 tbsp. apple cider vinegar
- 3 tbsp. apple juice
- 6 finely ground cloves
- Flip-cap bottles or foaming bottles to dispense

In a small grinder or blender, mix all ingredients on low for 30 seconds. Wet the hair with warm water and shampoo the mixture into the hair well. Rinse with warm water. Cover and refrigerate leftovers. Discard after three days!

Recipe 6: Shine

Fragrant and lively, try this recipe to add shine to your hair:

- ¼ cup distilled water
- 2 tbsp. dried rosemary
- ¼ cup liquid castile soap—try lemon!
- 2 tbsp. sweet almond oil
- ¼ tsp. lemon essential oil
- Flip-cap bottles or foaming bottles to dispense

Boil the distilled water, then add rosemary, and steep until fragrant. Strain leaves and let cool. Mix remaining ingredients, add to water, and stir well. Store in a bottle. Use as you would any shampoo and be sure to rinse well.

Recipe 7: Rejuvenate

This is a great shampoo for any hair type. You will need:

- ¼ cup distilled water
- 3 tbsp. rosemary
- 1 tbsp. lemongrass
- 2 tsp. tea tree oil
- 1 tsp. vanilla essential oil
- ¼ cup liquid castile soap—I use unscented, but you can choose your favorite
- Flip-cap bottles or foaming bottles to dispense

Boil distilled water, add rosemary and lemongrass (in tea strainer if you have it), and steep until fragrant (about 20–30 minutes). Strain leaves and let cool.

Mix the tea tree oil and vanilla into the water. Add soap.

Store in a bottle. Let the shampoo cool, and then place the top on tightly. Use as you would any shampoo, and be sure to rinse well.

Recipe 8: Yummy

I can't resist the alluring smell of this luxurious shampoo. You will need:

- ¼ cup distilled water
- ¼ cup liquid castile soap—I use unscented, but you can choose your favorite
- 2 tsp. jojoba oil
- 10 drops vanilla essential oil
- 10 drops coconut fragrance oil
- Flip-cap bottles or foaming bottles to dispense

Mix together all the ingredients. Store in a bottle. Use as you would any shampoo, and be sure to rinse well. Try not to drink this one. It smells so good!

Recipe 9: Dry

This is a great in-between treatment for hair, if you're helping someone who can't wash their hair on their own, or for removing dirt and oil from the hair when fresh water in unavailable. You will need:

- ¼ cup oatmeal
- 1 tsp. crushed lavender or other fragrant herb
- 1 tsp. baking soda

Grind ingredients together with a mortar and pestle, small grinder, or place in a baggie and crush with a rolling pin.

Sprinkle enough of the mixture to cover all hair, and massage for 5 minutes before it is brushed out.

This could be made in bulk and stored in a cool, dry environment.

Recipe 10: No Shampoo

Though there are already plenty of Instructables that cover this topic, I thought my list wouldn't be complete without including the simplest way to get clean, healthy hair. You will need:

- 1 tsp. baking soda
- Apple cider vinegar
- 4 oz. water

Put 1 tsp. baking soda in a cup or mug to take into the shower with you. In another cup, pour about 1 oz. (⅛ cup) apple cider vinegar.

When you get into the shower, fill the baking soda cup with about ¼ cup water. Apply this to your roots only; work it in and let it sit for a minute.

Then begin to gently scrub your scalp, stimulating blood flow and cleaning out your pores. This will actually stimulate hair growth.

Lastly, scrub the back of your skull and your temples/sideburns. This will result in less grease and more growth.

Rinse!

Follow by adding about ¼ cup water to the cup of vinegar. Pour this over the ends of your hair, let it sit for a minute, and then rinse it out.

No Shampoo Troubleshooting

There may be a transition period from two weeks to two months depending on the person. Here are a few tips:

If your hair becomes frizzy, try using less baking soda or leaving it on for a shorter period of time. Adding honey may also help.

If your hair becomes greasy, try using less apple cider vinegar, switching to lemon or lime juice, leaving out the honey, and/or using a comb instead of a brush. Also, make sure you're applying the apple cider vinegar to just the ends of your hair.

If your scalp itches, try the following essential oils: tea tree, lavender, or rosemary. If your hair becomes dry, try a tiny bit of oil (any oil, I use olive) smoothed on the bottom of your hair.

Have fun and enjoy!

Home Remedy for Burns

By suvarna Lakshmi

www.instructables.com/id/Home-Remedy-for-Burns/

This recipe is a home remedy for burns. This will help in healing the burns speedily and also remove the burn marks from the skin

Step 1: Ingredients

Only two ingredients are required: an aloe vera leaf and 1 tsp. of turmeric.

Step 2: Method

Clean the aloe vera leaf and remove sides and skin. With the help of a knife, collect the aloe vera gel. Mix the gel with turmeric to make a fine paste. Your aloe vera gel paste is ready. Apply this paste on burns.

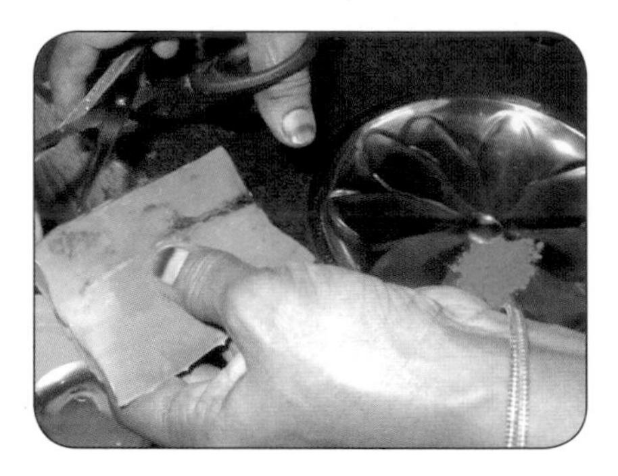

Make Your Skin Glow with Sandalwood Paste

By roopal05

www.instructables.com/id/Make-your-skin-glow-sandalwood-paste/

Sandalwood has inherent properties that soothe skin, lighten dark spots, enhance skin glow, and even out the skin's complexion.

Turmeric provides disinfectant properties.

When mixed together you are left with an unbeatable recipe nature has granted us.

Step 1: Ingredients

- 2 tbsp. sandalwood powder/stick
- 1 pinch turmeric powder
- A few drops of milk, if your skin is not oily.

Step 2: Instructions

Make a paste of sandalwood powder and turmeric in water using a mortar and pestle or a stone. If you don't have oily skin, add a few drops of milk. Apply on face for 20 minutes or until it dries completely. Wash your face. Feel the beautiful you.

Remedy for Losing Your Voice: Cayenne Cure

By Holly Mann

www.instructables.com/id/Remedy-for-Losing-Your-Voice-Cayenne-Cure/

In 2009, my son and I both contracted the H1N1 Swine Flu and were sick for a long time. Somewhere in the midst of illness I lost my voice. I literally could not talk and tried every cure I could find online to fix my problem so my little son could hear me again. Nothing worked until I tried this.

It is a very simple cure, but not for the weak minded! If you're afraid to do this I don't blame you, but it's all in your mind. If I can do this without vomiting, you can too (I hope). All you need is cayenne pepper.

Step 1: Mix Water and Cayenne

Take a small glass and pour in about ¼ teaspoon of cayenne pepper. Add a few tablespoons of warm to hot water to the cup and mix it around the best you can.

Step 2: Gargle

Now gargle with it and spit it out. You may need to do it a couple of times for it to work, or you may be fine after the first try. All I know is that my voice came back right away. It wasn't 100% back, but it was at least 70% better than before. And if hours later my voice started to go away again, I would do this again and it would be back. This really worked for me. Don't swallow the stuff, and be careful to not get it on your lips. It will tingle or burn!

CONVERSION TABLES

One person's inch is another person's centimeter. Instructables projects come from all over the world, so here's a handy reference guide that will help keep your project on track.

Measurement								
	1 Millimeter	1 Centimeter	1 Meter	1 Inch	1 Foot	1 Yard	1 Mile	1 Kilometer
Millimeter	1	10	1,000	25.4	304.8	—	—	—
Centimeter	0.1	1	100	2.54	30.48	91.44	—	—
Meter	0.001	0.01	1	0.025	0.305	0.91	—	1,000
Inch	0.04	0.39	39.37	1	12	36	—	—
Foot	0.003	0.03	3.28	0.083	1	3	—	—
Yard	—	0.0109	1.09	0.28	033	1	—	—
Mile	—	—	—	—	—	—	1	0.62
Kilometer	—	—	1,000	—	—	—	1.609	1

Volume										
	1 Milliliter	1 Liter	1 Cubic Meter	1 Tea spoon	1 Table-spoon	1 Fluid Ounce	1 Cup	1 Pint	1 Quart	1 Gallon
Milliliter	1	1,000	—	4.9	14.8	29.6	—	—	—	—
Liter	0.001	1	1,000	0.005	0.015	0.03	0.24	0.47	0.95	3.79
Cubic Meter	—	0.001	1	—	—	—	—	—	—	0.004
Teaspoon	0.2	202.9	—	1	3	6	48	—	—	—
Tablespoon	0.068	67.6	—	0.33	1	2	16	32	—	—
Fluid Ounce	0.034	33.8	—	0.167	0.5	1	8	16	32	—
Cup	0.004	4.23	—	0.02	0.0625	0.125	1	2	4	16
Pint	0.002	2.11	—	0.01	0.03	0.06	05	1	2	8
Quart	0.001	1.06	—	0.005	0.016	0.03	0.25	.05	1	4
Gallon	—	0.26	264.17	0.001	0.004	0.008	0.0625	0.125	0.25	1

Spice Index

Ginger

Nutmeg

Paprika

Pepper

Sage

Turmeric

Vanilla